CHOICES

Stopping Abuse in Intimate Relationships

Margy and Denny Hendershot

DENTON CONSULTING COMPANY
P.O. Box 247
Loveland, OH 45140

ISBN: 0-9629030-0-0

ACKNOWLEDGEMENTS

The calligraphy for this book was provided by PEN & INK, Hamilton, Ohio.

The artwork was done by a wonderful artist named Patricia Lynch from Cincinnati, Ohio.

We are grateful for permission to adapt and reprint the Iceberg model and exercise. This permission was graciously given by John Gray, the author of *WHAT YOU FEEL YOU CAN HEAL*.

Dave Petty, a very creative Indianapolis musician allowed us to reprint his song *The Razor's Edge*.

Our business manager, friend, consultant, graphics designer, jack-of-all-trades, Dave Eversmann has been invaluable. His patience and good humor tided him well as he fielded many inquiries about this long-delayed book. Thank you so much.

Finally, we wish to acknowledge Jamie, Jacob, Rachel, Katie, Joey, Kira, Gabbie, Courtland, Alex, Raymond, Crystal Water—all the little ones who have inspired us to work for a better world for them to grow up in. This book is part of our effort.

■

I wish to acknowledge my profound debt to my therapist, Larry Leitner. You promised me blood, sweat, tears, pain and freedom—and you delivered. Your love and faith in me allowed me to leave the prison of my fears and become a real person in the world. You lived relationship with me; what I have not learned is due to my stubbornness, not your ineptitude.

To Denny, my husband, my lover, my friend. You love me the way I am—a fact that continues to astound me. You have created the safe space I have needed to grow and then pushed my growing edges just enough. My life is infinitely fuller because you are in it.

To Randy, my son; I am bonded to you for life. I understand your need to individuate and I struggle with the distance between us that that necessitates. I am proud to be your Mom, and am giving it my best shot.

To my sister, Betty, and her husband Dean. Your support through some very lean times has not been forgotten. I am grateful for my connections to you.

To my first real friend, Bruce Pomeranz. We meet not often, but well.

To my new friend Mary Jo Lee. Validation from one as clear, congruent, and authentic as you is valuable indeed.

These connections, along with my work with injured men who injure others, give meaning to my life. I am very grateful.

Margy

■

To Margy, my wife. The long hours working and talking about this book have been enriching and fun. I am looking forward to our future together.

To my octogenarian father, W.L. (Curly) Hendershot, who never ceases to amaze me with his willingness and ability to change. The lessons I have learned from you are too numerous to count.

To my children: Marc, Greg and Marcie, and Jeff—in appreciation for your honesty in just being who you are.

To my grandchildren: Jamie and Jacob, you are the reason I do this work.

Denny

PREFACE

This book is the culmination of seven years work with groups of men who batter. It represents our continuing struggle to develop material and ways of presenting it so it can be of the most benefit to men who are struggling to change their lives.

This book is intended for use by these men; it is written very much in the vernacular we have used with success in our groups. Along the way, many clients have asked for written materials to share with their partners. Many of them report that their partners have also found the material helpful.

There is little fluff in this book; we generally have contact with our clients for a very short time; each segment must be maximally impactful.

This book is not a theoretical treatise; rather, it is hands-on information that gives a man the tools he needs to change his life for the better.

Working with these men evokes the full range of human emotion: horror, fear, pain, despair, joy, excitement, and sadness. It is very challenging work and has forced us to grow in ways we could not foresee. We are grateful to the men; they have taught us much about humanity and ourselves.

DEDICATION

This book is dedicated to the hundreds of men
who have allowed us to touch their lives.
We have been changed for the better by the contact.
We thank you.

TABLE OF CONTENTS

INTRODUCTION

Abuse in intimate relationships. There is a sadness, and sometimes bewilderment, when one thinks about those words. We invest in intimate relationships in order to fulfill some of our deepest psychological needs—to be cared for as we really are, to feel that we are important and matter to someone, to share our best selves, to grow, to gain some security in what feels like a very shaky world. We need those things for ourselves; we intend to provide them for our partners. How do we end up so far away from that goal in a place where hurt, fear, and rage prevail?

This book will provide some answers to that question. In those answers are the tools that will make it possible for you to choose a different path. Some of the material will make good sense to you; some may seem like total bullshit. There are many different answers because there are many different paths to abusive relationships. Choose the closest "fit" for you and adapt it as you need to. Ignore the rest. Do pay attention to your natural resistance to change. A good approach is to remind yourself that what you are doing isn't working. What have you got to gain by trying something new?

You may feel that it is not fair; why should you be the one that has to make changes? In the picture on the following page, the man is insisting that the fireplace give him some warmth—then he will give it the log. Don't let your pride or stubbornness condemn you to the cold.

> *You can survive on your own.*
> *You can grow stronger on your own.*
> *You can even prevail on your own.*
> *But you cannot become human on your own.*
>
> *Frederick Buechner*

Figure 1
FIREPLACE ILLUSTRATION

THE TRAIL OF TEARS

One who sets out in a relationship is really a person walking along an unfamiliar path in strange territory. The path is not straight, has many forks and is rarely marked. To add to the difficulty, our traveler may have learned to ignore his innate sense of direction and to respond to the feedback the trail does offer (the consequences of his choices) in ways that lead him further astray. He may become so bewildered that he forgets his original goal and becomes truly lost. For this wanderer, the journey seems random and chaotic; an overhead view of his choices reveals discernible phases.

Phase I looks and feels "normal". The honeymoon is over and one has to get back to work. This phase is marked not by what he does, but what he fails to do. Typical choices include being preoccupied with other interests (e.g., the job or hobbies), taking one's partner for granted, not taking the time to listen, not making the relationship a priority. No big, dramatic points here, only small seemingly harmless decisions.

Phase II often feels like a "natural" response to Phase I. It is characterized by withdrawal, withholding, and the walling off of both your partner's and your own feelings. Behaviors might include the silent treatment, refusing to acknowledge or talk about problems, staying away from home.

These are the neglect phases. The damage occurs not because of what you do, but because of the things you don't do.

In **Phase III** one of the partners attempts to correct the situation. However, instead of recognizing that he has chosen the wrong fork in the road and needs to retrace his steps, our traveler attempts to change the present landscape to match his original goal. Controlling, manipulating, and attempting to change one's partner seem like the logical tools for such a job. These efforts are doomed to fail because the task itself is impossible. This failure increases the anger level.

Phase IV is characterized by the indirect expression of this anger through such methods as criticism, sarcasm, snide remarks, blaming, nagging, forgetfulness, tardiness and a myriad of other behaviors designed to "pay back" injuries without a direct confrontation. Responses to such behaviors are predictably negative and often serve as a "lead-in" to Phase V—open verbal arguments.

Phase V arguments can range from cold, logical, "civilized" disagreements to loud, screaming, "no-holds-barred" shouting matches., There are many verbally abusive behaviors including name-calling, swearing at, mocking, put-downs, bringing up the past, inflicting intentional injuries in vulnerable places.

Movement into **Phase VI** is marked by physical violence. Such violence is often a response to feeling powerless. For the female partner, this feeling may come from her perception that her words have little or no effect. A man is socialized not to show that he is injured. A woman often interprets this lack of reaction as her failure to make an impact. This adds to her fury and she may respond by hitting. (Studies show that women hit as often as men do.)

Women often initiate the hitting because our society gives them implied permission to do so. For example, girls are instructed to slap "fresh" boys and many a movie heroine has hit the hero. Reactions to such behaviors on the part of women range from open encouragement to conveyed messages of "she's so cute when she's mad". The woman never appears to be ashamed of such actions, her friends are not appalled, no one feels a need to talk to her about her temper problem.

For the male partner, the powerless feeling may come from his awareness that he is getting too angry—and that he is unable to find a way to get his partner to stop. He may say all the words he knows to get her to back down and give him some room to cool off—and she responds by escalating and moving closer. (Men often interpret this behavior as meaning "she must want to get hit"). Men are socialized not to hit women and generally feel ashamed and appalled at such reactions.

At this phase the ability to inflict roughly equal damage gets lost and the advantage swings to the male partner. Men are typically bigger and stronger than women, their bones are four times heavier and their upper body strength is much more developed. Even though women hit as much as men do, 95% of all injuries happen to women. This phase may also mark the intervention of the legal system as it is illegal for one adult to hit another in this country.

Phases I through VI are considered expressive abuse. This means that such behaviors are chosen to express feelings of pain, fear, anger, and rage.

Because of the physical damage differential, **Phase VII** may be characterized by less hitting because the man can shift to meaningful threats. However, if the female partner is angry enough, even threats or the remembrance of past injuries won't keep her from the mutual escalation process. If the threats are successful, a very different psychological process may begin. Having discovered that he can make his partner do as he wishes if he makes her afraid, the man may begin to use threats and violence to control her. Phase VII is thus the bridge-over phase into instrumental violence.

Phase VIII—instrumental violence is virtually always carried out by the male partner. It is violence (and threats of violence) used as an instrument to control his partner's behavior. He may or may not be angry; he is deliberate and very much in control. His need for control becomes overwhelming and his level of violence is so terrifying that his partner lives in real fear for her life.

She may develop battered woman's syndrome—a psychological state similar to that occurring to long-term prisoners-of-war. Such women occasionally kill their husbands, believing that there is no other choice.

More often, they live in terror, helpless victims of their partner's rage and their own survival reactions.

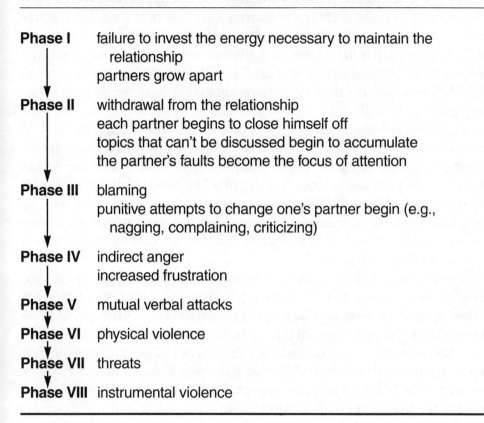

Figure 2
CONTINUUM OF ABUSE IN RELATIONSHIPS

Phase I failure to invest the energy necessary to maintain the relationship
partners grow apart

Phase II withdrawal from the relationship
each partner begins to close himself off
topics that can't be discussed begin to accumulate
the partner's faults become the focus of attention

Phase III blaming
punitive attempts to change one's partner begin (e.g., nagging, complaining, criticizing)

Phase IV indirect anger
increased frustration

Phase V mutual verbal attacks

Phase VI physical violence

Phase VII threats

Phase VIII instrumental violence

CONSEQUENCES

Abusive behaviors are choices. People sometimes minimize the damage caused by these choices. A closer look at the reality of these consequences presents a grim picture.

The neglect phases (I and II) result in a feeling that the two of you have "fallen out of love" and serve as a lead-in to the expressive phases.

Expressive phases III through V bring unhappiness, betrayals, divorces, and deep mutual wounds. They may also be a prelude to physical violence—phase VI.

At Phase VI, the abuse becomes a crime—a crime called battering. The legal consequences vary. They may include fines, court costs, jail-time, restitution, restraining or protective orders, probation, or mandated services such as counseling groups. The personal consequences of being arrested include embarrassment, increased stress, criminal records, job loss and loss of status in the community. Battering has not always been illegal; however, the consequences are so serious that most legislatures have established battering as a subcategory of assault. Battering occurs within an intimate relationship. It is the existence of the relationship that differentiates battering from assault. The relationship is also the reason that the consequences of battering are somewhat different from the con-sequences of assault.

Battering is lethal. Lethal means that people die. Each year several thousand women in this country die as a result of domestic violence. Most of them die in fights—*fights just like the ones you have.* A woman is punched, or pushed, or shoved. She hits her head on the corner of a sharp table and she dies. She lands crooked when she hits the wall or falls down the stairs, breaks her spine—and she dies. A ring punctures her eyeball and the shock kills her. It happens several thousand time a year, *in fights just like yours.*

The partners of these women are charged with manslaughter because they did not mean to kill. They go to jail, serving an average of 25 years to life. Add 25 years to your age right now. That is how old you could be the next time you see freedom if your fights escalate to violence.

Almost exactly the same number of men are killed in domestic vio-lence arguments each year. Most of them are killed with weapons—stabbed, shot or hit with heavy objects. Their partners also go to jail for most of the remainder of their adult lives.

The children in these families? Fifty percent of the time, the children watch the killing. Many of these children then end up in foster-care. Some adjust (no child ever really is OK after watching one parent kill another); many are not manageable in foster-care. These latter children are very angry at being deprived of their parents. Their rage is likely to result in rejections from several homes before they end up in some type of institution. A disproportionate number of these children end up in prison. *Kids just like yours.*

These are not the only domestic violence caused deaths. In 60% of all homicides committed by teen-age boys, the victim is the man who is beating on the boy's mother—the dad, step-dad, or boyfriend. If you have ever seen your mother hit, you know how these young men feel.

These teens throw their lives away. The chances of a young man getting out of the juvenile justice system with a homicide on his record and being able to find work are very slim. Many of these young men turn to crime and end up in prison.

Further deaths can be chalked up to the increased suicide rate among both partners in these relationships. About one-third of the time when the man kills himself, he takes his partner and sometimes his children with him.

Battering is lethal. Women die. Men die. Children die. Families die.

Battering also does a great deal of physical damage, mostly to women. As we have said before, the average man is larger and taller than his partner, his bones are heavier, and his upper body muscles are more developed. As a result, he is able to inflict more injuries and more severe injuries than his partner can. His ability to hurt her so much may terrify her—a situation that is rarely reversed. Most of the women who are treated at emergency rooms are treated for injuries inflicted by their intimate partners. Just as in the deaths caused by domestic violence, in most cases the men involved do not intend to cause so much damage. They are often surprised and appalled when they cool down enough to see what they have done. At that point, it is, of course, too late. Even the most sincere apologies are poor compensation for broken bones, bumps, bruises, cuts and the other multitude of injuries inflicted during fights.

The psychological damage for everyone involved in domestic violence is horrendous.

Every time a woman is hit by someone who loves her, she loses a piece of self-esteem. There is a part of her that begins to believe that there must be something wrong with her that someone who loves her can treat her so badly. It becomes easier and easier for her to believe that she is at fault and that she somehow *deserves* to be beaten. If the battering continues long enough, she may lose so much self-respect that she develops battered woman's syndrome, a condition similar to a prisoner-of-war. Such a woman has become an empty shell of a person who is unable to stand up for herself.

The damage to the batterer is also severe. Every time you allow yourself to lose control and hit the woman you love, you lose a piece of your own self-esteem. As your self-esteem gets eroded away it becomes easier and easier to choose violence, leading to the instrumental end of the continuum, where a man no longer recognizes himself. Your own experience may verify this. The first time a man hits his partner, he generally feels like shit. He says to her, and to himself, that it will never happen again. He feels so bad that he really means it. *The next time it is a little easier.*

Do you think the children are unaffected by the abuse in your relationship? Many studies would refute that. The most obvious level of injury is the actual physical abuse of children. The statistics are very grim. A child in a home with violent parents has a *1500%* greater chance of being abused than a child in a safer environment. About one-third of all partners who abuse each other also abuse the children. Very high risk children include babies who pick up parental stress and become whiny and clinging, toddlers who don't know enough or aren't fast enough to avoid the combatants and older children who step in between in an attempt to stop the fight.

Another less obvious level is the psychological damage. A child's emotional development is profoundly dependent on the safety and nurturance provided by you and your partner. Healthy emotional development requires:

- nurturance
- support
- structure
- supervision
- peace
- security
- a sense of what is normal

A child growing up in a home with domestic violence or abuse is deprived of many or all of these. He lives in a world characterized by:

- an increased risk of injury
- an increased risk of being abused
- a disrupted life
- stress caused by background anger
- fear
- anxiety
- confusion
- anger
- insecurity
- terror
- powerlessness
- guilt

The consequences of such deprivation and negative environment can be seen in a broad range of problems. These include:

Physical Symptoms
- psychosomatic complaints
- stress disorders
- increased suicide risk
- weight and eating problems
- sleeping difficulties
- bed-wetting
- excessive crying or screaming
- stuttering
- nail-biting or hair-pulling

Emotional Difficulties
- low self-esteem
- self-blame
- limited frustration tolerance
- poor impulse control
- "martyr" role-taking
- depression
- "parental" role-taking
- unmet dependencies making one high risk for:
  — sexual acting-out
  — drugs and alcohol abuse
  — running away from home
  — peer pressure

Behavior Problems
- being distracted and inattentive in school
- being truant
- pre-delinquent and delinquent behaviors
- isolation
- development of deception patterns: lying, stealing, cheating
- assaultiveness, fighting
- passivity
- becoming withdrawn
- being clingy
- temper tantrums

Your children also use your home to develop a model of the world, i.e., a way to make sense of what happens, how to determine what is important, how to relate to other people. Some of the lessons learned from parents who abuse each other:

- All power belongs to the wrong-doer.
- Nice people finish last.
- Violence is the basis for power and control.
- Might makes right.
- People who love you also hurt you.
- Violence is an acceptable solution to problems.
- Abuse is normal.
- One is not responsible for the quality of his life—you can always blame someone else for your problems.
- Mistrust the opposite sex.
- Use either passive or aggressive strategies to solve interpersonal conflict.

These lessons begin to show up when the children attempt to establish intimate relationships for themselves. Studies show that one-third of all girls in high school are being hit by their boyfriends. ("When you love someone, you take the bad with the good.") Of course, this means one boy of every three is hitting his girlfriend. These two then marry each other and start the cycle all over again.

Choosing abuse means choosing to lose—your relationship, your partner, your family, your self-respect, your freedom, and perhaps even your life.

No one gets involved in relationships to be abused or to be abusive. Those choices often come from having poor tools, or no tools, to choose from. It is our hope that this book will provide you with some workable better choices for you and your family.

> The highest reward for
> any man's labor is not
> what he gets for it,
> but what he becomes by it.
>
> Brock Bell

SECTION I
ANGER & ANGER MANAGEMENT

ANGER

The first segment of this book is devoted to anger and anger control because much of the abuse in relationships occurs when one or both partners are angry. Anger in a relationship is generally not the first feeling that you experience.

The model that we use to talk about this is an iceberg. Anger is like the tip of the iceberg, it is very small in proportion to that which is below the surface. The feeling closest to the surface and easiest to get in touch with is *pain*. Generally, a man who is angry at his partner is aware of what was done or said that felt hurtful to him. Consider the last time you were angry at your partner—how did she hurt you?

Figure 3
ANGER ICEBERG

Fear is another *submerged* feeling. Fear is generally deeper—sometimes so deep it is out of our awareness—and is difficult to touch. It may be the fear of losing control, fear of losing your partner, fear of failing or any of the many universal fears that we all experience.

Another component of the iceberg is *guilt and responsibility.* No one likes to feel guilty and it is much easier to blame our partners for all of the difficulties. At the same time, we do know that one cannot fight by himself.

The other major part of the structure is *love and caring.* If we did not love our partners and care for them, we wouldn't get as angry as we do. Think about it. If a stranger came up to you in a bar and called you the names your wife called you, you would blow her off. It hurts because it is your partner; someone you love and who you want to love you.

Before we discuss how these submerged feelings erupt as anger, take a few minutes to complete the following exercise. Fill out the sentence stems for each component. Allow at least five minutes for each. Write down whatever comes up. Don't be concerned about the importance of the item.

Figure 2
ICEBERG EXERCISE

Anger and Blame

I don't like it when. . .

I resent. . .

I'm fed up with. . .

I'm tired of. . .

I want to strike out when. . .

Hurt and Sadness

I feel sad when. . .

I feel hurt because. . .

I feel awful because. . .

I feel disappointed because. . .

I feel like crying when I think. . .

I feel so hurt that you. . .

I feel betrayed when you. . .

Fear and Insecurity

I feel afraid when. . .

I am afraid that. . .

I feel scared because. . .

I am scared when. . .

I become afraid when I think that. . .

I feel scared when I remember. . .

My greatest fear about us is. . .

Guilt and Responsibility

I am sorry that. . .

I am sorry for. . .

Please forgive me for. . .

I did not mean to. . .

I made a mistake when. . .

I know I was wrong for. . .

I really regret that I. . .

Love, Forgiveness, Understanding

I love you because. . .

I love when. . .

Thank you for. . .

I understand that. . .

I forgive you for. . .

I want to work it out because. . .

I want for us to. . .

Note: This exercise and model is adapted and used with permission from *WHAT YOU FEEL; YOU CAN HEAL* by John Gray. See the bibliography for the complete reference.

Were you surprised to find all the feelings there?

This is a good exercise to do *anytime* you're angry. It tends to put the anger into better perspective. Another suggestion is to ask your partner to do the exercise, then exchange. Keep in mind that it takes a lot of courage to share some of these feelings. Don't be hard on yourself or on her if it doesn't feel safe enough yet to be this vulnerable. You are the only one who can judge the safety of the relationship for you. She is the only one who can make that judgement for herself.

> *Anger is often a substitute for knowledge;*
>
> *violence a defense against truth.*
>
> Dr. William Arthur Ward

If we were to ask you to tell us about the last time you got angry, you would probably answer with an example like this, "She did X or didn't do X and made me mad." Most of us experience the process of getting angry like that—in part because getting angry can happen very quickly. The process of getting angry is really not that simple. Let's break it down so we can look at it in detail.

To start with, we have two stressed people in a special relationship. Each of you brings to the situation your personal history (as you have interpreted it), your present needs, and your expectations for the future. Each of these is a kind of filter that effects what you experience. Another way to think of these factors is to compare them to old tapes that play automatically; sometimes even without our being aware of them. Each of you also functions under chronic stress, much of which is so "normal", it is not recognized as stressful. Your physical system recognizes it, however, and your body chemistry reflects that knowledge.

The relationship? It is the riskiest relationship two adults can have. We can choose to damage each other more deeply than is possible in any other context.

The first step is the occurrence of an event that we'll call a *trigger*. The event can be external (your partner forgot to write down a check she used, so you cannot balance the checkbook) or internal (you remember that snide remark your partner made about you at the party last night). *Anything* can be a trigger; from a large event (finding your partner in bed with someone else) to a small event (your partner forgot to buy more of "your" toothpaste and you have to use that yukky blue gel); an on-going struggle (your partner fails to discipline the children "right"), or a first-time event (your underwear is now pink because your partner washed them with a red towel).

It would really be handy if we could draw up a list of events that serve as triggers for anger. We could then discuss how to deal with each one and so *disarm* them. Unfortunately, such a list is impossible since *any* event can serve as a trigger.

Think of some of the arguments you've had, fights caused by really trivial events. The authors once had a major blow-up while disagreeing about whether water molecules ever break up into atoms. Now *that* is an issue *obviously* worth detonating an explosion.

Events themselves are not actually the triggers, it is the *meanings* that we give these events that determine whether or not we are willing to go to war. Some typical anger evoking meanings are:

Event X means that I am:
- being pushed around
- being misled, betrayed, used, disappointed
- being hurt
- being attacked
- not cared for
- not important to her
- not valued as I am
- being taken for granted
- being insulted or put down
- being treated like I am not good enough
- being looked down on
- being treated as a subordinate
- losing

The common thread running through these meanings is the feeling of loss of control. A response to this feeling may be anger, a signal from your system that something isn't right. Anger alerts you to the problem and mobilizes your energy to help you deal with it.

The analogy we like to use is that anger is your system's smoke alarm—obviously a useful tool to have. Now that we are aware that there is a problem, and have gotten charged up to deal with it, what do we do?

> *. . . Some of the things that people suffer most from are the things they tell themselves that are not true.*
>
> Elvin Semrad

Ignoring Anger

There are two popular strategies for dealing with anger—ignoring it or expressing it. One of the methods used to ignore anger is to *become depressed*. The person who chooses this method hears the smoke alarm go off and puts in ear plugs. This strategy does stop the noise; however, it also stops music, laughter, people reaching out, etc. This option prevents fights and allows you to feel like a victim, or the good guy, in the situation. It nonverbally tells people not to expect too much from you or to ask you for much. It also prevents intimacy by turning all of the energy inward so there is none available to connect with someone else.

Some depressed people continue to function, leading grey, meaningless lives. Others begin to despair, feeling that life is filled with too much pain and that is no hope for the future. At this point, suicide may begin to feel like the best choice available. Most people who choose suicide are depressed.

Another choice for ignoring anger is to *change it into physical symptoms*. The person who chooses this method, hears the smoke alarm go off and channels the energy activated by its noise into activity. Most often he chooses to become a workaholic, but other options could include hobbies, sports, yard-work, etc. Our physical system is not designed to function under such continual stress. Symptoms such as ulcers and high blood pressure begin to appear. Ignoring such symptoms can lead to very dramatic system breakdowns, such as heart attacks. These are the men who die on the run at age 35.

A third method for ignoring anger is to *develop sexual problems*. In choosing this method, the person hears the smoke alarm go off and then attempts to will himself not to respond. This technique requires enormous energy and leaves little left over for other expressive systems. The sexual energy system literally runs out of steam, resulting in impotence, frigidity, or lack of interest. Since our sexuality is part of our definition of ourselves, a shut-down in this area can evoke feelings of failure and shame, which may in turn fuel depression.

The most popular method to ignore anger is *stuffing*. The person who chooses this method hears the smoke alarm go off and then tries to convince himself that the noise really doesn't bother him at all. Stuffing prevents small fights and keeps you from feeling petty. In choosing this option you may say things like, "It wasn't worth having a fight over" or "It's easier to just let it go, it really is no big deal". This choice also prevents intimacy from developing. Each time it is used another brick is mortared into place in the the wall between the two partners.

Stuffers generally do not want their partners to know that a fire has been lit so they continually shove the hot coals under the carpet. Quite predictably, the carpet catches fire and during the ensuing fight all the coals are dragged out. These blow-ups can be quite intense and the damage from the heat is rarely totally reparable. After the stuffer blows up a few times, those around him learn that this is his style and they develop a healthy fear of him. Of course, this guarantees that no intimacy can develop since one cannot be intimate with someone he fears.

The overall impact of the strategy of ignoring anger is to *create emotional distance* and to *weaken the bonds* in the relationship.

Expressing Anger

The other major strategy for dealing with anger is to express it either *directly or indirectly*. Those who choose indirect methods of expression hear the smoke alarm, then hang a blanket over it to muffle the sound which then leaks out around the edges. One indirect method is the use of passive-aggressive behaviors such as *forgetting* to fill the car with gas, *accidentally* flushing the john while your partner is in the shower, or being chronically late. Indirect anger also shows up in *sexual behaviors* such as flirting, hurtful comparisons, or "not so discreet" affairs.

It is likely that the most common indirect choice is the development of a *critical attitude* which is then expressed in tone of voice, small jabs, pointed looks, or little snipes.

Such indirect expressions of anger erode the caring in the relationship and lead to misery for both partners.

You can also choose to express anger directly—either *physically* or by *venting*. Those who choose this option hear the smoke alarm, then rip that sucker off the wall and attempt to beat the fire out with it. Physical actions lead to destruction of property, others, or self.

The other direct method, venting, is the process of dumping your garbage on your partner with words. This option relieves all the stress and tension in one's body. It makes you feel powerful and strong. It gets everything out in the open and leaves no doubt about how you feel. It also damages your self-esteem, injures the people you care about and destroys your meaningful relationships. Since it is often experienced by your partner as an attack, it can lead to physical violence and is unlikely to be tolerated over time. Venting is often the result of choosing to be right rather than choosing to be happy.

The overall effect of expressing your anger directly is the destruction of the bonds of the relationship.

These appear to be the most common choices made when people are angry. Did you find yours? Your partner's? Most people have favored a choice so often that it is now a habit. This leaves the energy used for choosing freed up to then deal with the consequences.

Over time we can start to believe that the consequences *are* the problem, completely forgetting that they are the *consequences*. For example: you choose to let your anger escalate to the point where you hit her. One of the consequences of this choice is that she stops doing caring things for you. (It's difficult to feel affectionate toward someone who hurts you.) You then spend your energy trying to get her to change—forgetting that her withdrawal is a consequence of your choice.

Others, perhaps hoping to avoid the consequences, treat their anger as a smorgasbord—sampling one, then another. A person might, for example, stuff for a while, then vent, then choose depression. This is rather like being offered only poisons to eat and choosing small amounts of each in hope that there will not be enough of any particular one to kill you. This strategy is not successful because it is the *amount* of toxicity that destroys; the types chosen make little difference.

There is another option. It is less commonly used, not because it is a poor choice, but because most people are unaware of its existence. That option is to treat your system's smoke alarm (the anger) exactly as you would treat the smoke alarms in your home. When the smoke alarm goes off in your house, there are certain steps that you follow.

Excellent choice

First you go to the alarm to see if there is a fire. If there is one, and it is small, you put it out. If the blaze is too large, you flee to safety. *Second,* if there is no fire, *YOU SHUT THE ALARM OFF.* If you didn't do this next, the noise would drive you crazy. *Third,* you check to find out what set off the alarm. Is there something burning on the stove? Is something smoldering in the walls? Does the alarm need new batteries? You always assume there is a good reason for the signal and work to remedy the situation so the alarm doesn't go off again.

You can choose to follow this procedure with your anger. In our lives, just as with our home smoke alarms, there are many more signals than there are actual fires. The only two actual fires that come to mind are: 1) an instance where you are in actual physical danger of being killed* and 2) a situation where the brakes on your parked car have somehow let go and the car has rolled over your child, pinning him under it. In these instances use your angry energy to "put out the fire", i.e., to save yourself or your child. These "real" fires are rare.

The next step is to *SHUT THE ALARM OFF.* When translated, this means *COOL OUT.* (The Control Break segment of this section will give you the tools to do that.) Trying to solve the problem while the alarm is going off is fruitless, tends to make the situation even noisier and more chaotic, and is often destructive. *COOL OUT FIRST.*

After cooling out, do some problem investigation and problem solving. Ideas about how to do this can be found in the Healing Section of this book.

The overall effect of this choice is to strengthen the bonds of the relationship.

On the following page, Figure 5 illustrates the strategies of anger and the results of these choices.

---

*Remember that the legal definition of self-defense is **very** specific. It requires that you have reason to believe that you are in danger of being killed and that you cannot get away. Even then, you are allowed to use only the force necessary to save yourself.

Figure 5
ANGER

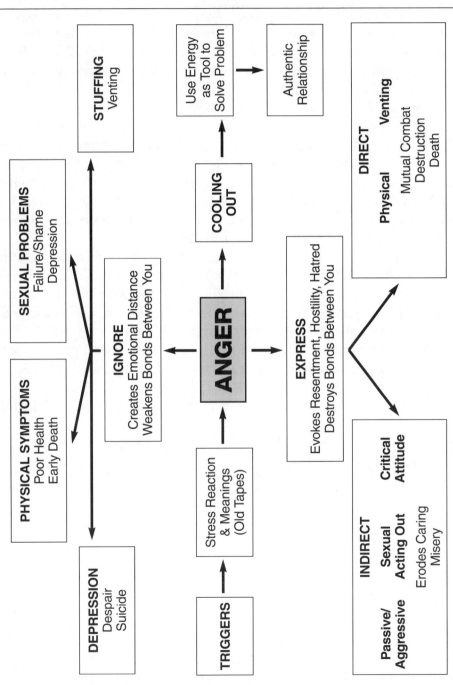

Of the seven deadly sins,
anger is probably the most fun.

To lick your wounds,
to smack your lips over grievances long past,
to roll over your tongue the prospect of
bitter confrontations still to come,
to savor to the last toothsome morsel
both the pain you are given, and the pain
you are giving back – in many ways,
it is a feast fit for a king.

The chief drawback is that what you
are wolfing down is yourself.

The skeleton at the feast is you.

Frederick Buechner

CONTROL BREAK

Control Break is the name we use for a set of tools designed to help you cool out. Some of them are easy to learn to use, others take more practice and skill. Each of them works; thousands of men we have counseled have attested to that! Choose the ones that feel most comfortable to you and then make a commitment to using them regularly. Over time the use of cooling out tools can begin to feel like a natural reaction.

Control breaks are choices. Before we describe these choices, we want to be clear about what type of tool a control break is.

Control breaks are *not:*
- ways to solve the problem causing the conflict
- ways to avoid talking about "hot" topics
- ways to dismiss your partner's concerns or feelings
- ways of changing your partner's behaviors, attitudes, or feelings

A control break is a choice to stop allowing one's anger to be acted out in abusive ways. It is a tool that you can use to insure that *you* are in charge of your anger. A control break is based on the assumption that when you are not angry, you do not want to hurt your partner. Choosing to take a control break means that you recognize that acting when you are angry is destructive to your partner, your relationship, and yourself.

You must be willing to give up the adrenaline rush that comes from letting anger get out of control. You must also give up the temporary feeling of power in exchange for the authentic power that comes from being in charge of yourself. Choosing to take a control break means choosing to grow up.

The Cycles of Arguments

One of the dynamics that makes it possible to choose to take a control break is that arguments have cycles. Arguments tend to happen the same way over and over, no matter what the argument is about. You know that sinking feeling you get in the pit of your stomach when you and your partner are about to head into really stormy waters? The feeling is a signal that the argument cycle has started. The cycle of your arguments may be somewhat different from the model presented next; however, you will very likely recognize this pattern.

Start with *two stressed people*. If the two of you were laying on the beach in Hawaii enjoying your new-won lottery millions, it is unlikely that you would have many fights. There is a physical reason for stress to be a big factor in fights. When a person is stressed his body chemistry changes. His system is trying to give him the necessary energy to fight or flee. Several body chemical levels change including the very same ones that change when a person gets angry. If you are carrying around a lot of stress (and most of us are), you are primed to get angry. (The Special Challenges segment of this book will discuss stress in greater detail.)

Add a trigger. The trigger sets off an old tape *which your system interprets as another stressor*. In response, your body chemistry begins to change and you begin to experience a physical reaction. You may begin to get hot or sweaty, your muscles begin to get pumped up, your attention narrows to concentrate on what your system interprets as a danger, all unnecessary body functions (such as the digestion of food) cease.

A trigger can be any event or even a memory of an event. The example we use as a trigger is to set the scene in the midwest, where you have had a typical winter day-cold, wet, and grey. You have been working all day at a job you do not like but are grateful to have since jobs are so scarce. They are laying off people at your plant, and you have some concern that your turn may be coming. You have not been able to follow the economists' advice; you do not have six month's salary in the bank. In fact, you are like all the rest of us, basically living from paycheck to paycheck.

On the way home, your car begins making a disturbing noise. You're thinking "What else can go wrong?". All you want to do is park your car in the garage and your body in a chair in front of the tube. You certainly want no more hassles. As you pull into the driveway the *final straw* is waiting. One of the children's tricycles is blocking your path. Now you've only asked this woman at least fourteen times not to let the kids leave their things in the driveway. She obviously doesn't give a damn about your feelings. You get mad.

You stamp into the house and *greet her with a shout*, "Damn it. How many times have I told you not to let the kids leave their toys in the driveway?". She sniffs your breath and *responds by shouting* at you for stopping with your buddies for a beer on the way home. The fight is on.

Each of you drags up all of the unresolved issues from the past, the loudness increases and the anger builds. Each side adds more weapons —criticism, name-calling, put-downs, sarcasm—an impressive array of techniques designed to injure the partner enough that he or she will surrender. Finally, one reaches the *last straw decision point*; the place where he says to himself, "This is the last straw. I can't take any more of this."

The next step is rage. Your system is so overloaded with stress chemicals that it responds as if this were a life-or-death struggle. The consequences no longer matter. Let's face it, if you were wrestling with a bengal tiger in your living room, would you be concerned about breaking a lamp? Think about the crazy things you've done (or said) while in a rage.

We've worked with men who have broken their hands when they punched walls, destroyed their own belongings, or handed their partners the phone, taunting them to call the police. How can you explain a woman who will get right up in her enraged partner's face and then taunt him to hit her, knowing she is going to be injured if he does? (No, she does not *want* to be hit, as is sometimes the man's interpretation.) Since we are not *actually* in a life-or-death struggle, this lack of concern for the consequences can lead to irreparable destruction.

Once the rage subsides, the tension is relieved and we may experience a *honeymoon period* during which we feel better than normal. For some troubled couples, these may be the only tension-free periods in the relationship, thus setting the stage for regular cycles of such battles. Unfortunately, the cost of achieving these temporary good feelings is very high—the destruction of relationships, families, even the individuals involved.

The pattern can be summarized like this:

- two stressed people
- another stressor
- verbal argument
- last straw decision
- RAGE
- honeymoon period

Such patterns become habitual ways of dealing with stress and conflict. As unresolved issues pile up, the time it takes to get from another stressor to RAGE may be very short and the honeymoon phase can disappear.

One of the keys to making control breaks work is an awareness that the further into the cycle you go before making a different choice, the harder it is to stop the cycle. This is because the rate of your body chemistry changes increases as the fight escalates. You, in effect, have fewer and fewer sane brain cells as you move into the battle. Look at the cycle again.

EASIER CHOICES—More Control of Thoughts, Feelings, Behaviors
Two stressed people
Another stressor
Verbal argument
DIFFICULT CHOICES—Less Control
Last straw decision
NO CHOICE—Rage

Keeping this in mind, we will start with the most difficult change choice, then work our way into easier techniques.

The last step at which you have a choice is immediately following the last straw decision point. If you wait until then, you have only one option, a time-out. People sometimes believe they already take time-outs. This is like believing that if you use a steak knife to pound in a nail it turns the knife into a hammer. Time-outs are very specific tools and work best if used in very specific ways.

Time-Outs

Time-outs work. Many men use them and find them effective. If the fight escalates to the last straw decision, TAKE A TIME-OUT.

Figure 6
TIME-OUTS

Step 1   Tell your partner you are taking a time-out. Do not just storm out of the house.

Step 2   Leave the house. It is not enough to go down the the basement or out to the garage; she will just follow you and the fight will continue.

Step 3   Leave for a specified period of time. We recommend one hour. Staying out all night or leaving for three days is not a time-out.

Step 4   Do something physical. We recommend taking a walk. Walking for an hour will help shift your body chemistry back to normal. **Do not** do something that is physical *and* aggressive such as hitting a punching bag or chopping wood. Research shows that this only makes one angrier. **Do not** drive. There are enough crazy drivers on the road. Stay out of your car. **Do not** go get a drink. Alcohol depletes a chemical called serotonin from your system. Serotonin's job is impulse-control. (Ever notice that drunks do crazy, impulsive things?) The last thing you need when you feel like punching your partner's face off is no impulse control. Go for a walk.

Step 5   After an hour, call her. There are two reasons for this. First, she needs to know that you have cooled down so she won't be frightened when you come home; second, when couples fight it is most common for both parties to escalate. She may be in a rage. If she is, don't go home. Tell her you'll give her some more time, call her in another hour. If she is still enraged, stay with your brother or best friend for the night. If you go home when she is still in a rage, you will get back into the fight, taking the chance that one of you will be hurt or killed.

Step 6   It is likely that she will also be cooled down. It is difficult to stay angry for an hour without someone to egg you on. If she is cooled out, give some ground. You do not need to lie or be manipulative; however you can own up to something you shouldn't have done. For example, "I shouldn't have slammed out of the house." The reason for giving some ground is that it lets the two of you step out of the "right versus wrong" trap and gives you both a place to stand so you can talk.

Step 7   If the two of you can talk about it *without* getting angry, do that. If not, set a time, e.g., tomorrow evening after we've both had a chance to recoup. Those who don't resolve arguments are doomed to repeat them.

Time-outs work. We highly recommend them. That said, we have some major reservations about time-outs.

First, the time span between the last straw decision and RAGE can be *very* short. You only have about two sane brain cells left so slipping into RAGE can be spectacularly easy.

Secondly, women often won't let men take a time-out. There are two reasons for this. One is that women are sometimes afraid that if you leave when you are angry, you won't come back. (Some of you pour gasoline on this fire by shouting "I'm leaving this damned house and never coming back" as you slam out the door.) If this is the case with your partner, you may be able to fix this by setting up the time-out ahead of time. Sit down with her at a time when you're not fighting. Explain to her that you want to set up a time-out because you care about her and don't want things to get violent between you. Tell her the plan—how long you'll be gone, where you will be walking, that you will call her before returning home, where you will stay if coming home is too risky. Negotiate the terms so that both of you can live with them.

The other reason women won't let men take time-outs is if a woman is already in a rage, she doesn't care about the consequences. If your partner won't let you leave because she is in a rage, *do not, under any circumstances, touch her.* There are several good reasons for this. You will have a domestic violence charge, you are stronger than normal when you are angry and may injure her, or she may escalate even further. If you are near rage and she hits you with something, the likelihood of your being able to back it down is not good. *BACK OFF.* Go take a cold shower, go out the back door, go out the bedroom window. *BACK OFF.* You have been socialized to never back down from a fight; very poor advice when you are struggling with your partner.

Our third reservation is that significant damage happens *before* time-outs, during the verbal argument. Most relationships are destroyed with words, not fists. The things that are said during these fights inflict damage that may never heal. Apologizing and explaining that you did not mean what you said does not heal the injury. In addition, verbal abuse sets up your partner as someone less than human—an easier target for abuse. It is much more difficult to be abusive to a real person than to a "bitch".

We recommend that you take a control break before you begin to verbally abuse each other. There are many ways to do this and they are easier to put into effect than are time-outs. The acronym we use to list some techniques is **CRUMBS**.

C Set up a **caring agreement**. Caring agreements state that the two of you will only discuss hot topics as long as you are both sitting down. If either of you stands up, there is a break so you can both cool down. Caring agreements allow each of you to monitor not only yourselves, but also your partner.

R Remind yourself of the importance of the **relationship**. Are you really willing to damage the bonds between you because of a trike in the driveway? How might you address this issue without being abusive?

U Successful couples—couples who stay together happily—learn to always aim for **understanding** before attempting to come to agreement. Be clear that you understand where she's coming from and why she feels that way *before* you try to explain your side.

M Monitor your breathing. If you find that you cannot take deep breaths, take a break. When you are angry, you tighten up and take only shallow breaths which your system interprets as a survival signal. It responds by pumping out more chemicals making you angrier still. Breathe.

B Be your **best** self. Asking for something as your best self is more likely to result in a positive response than if you come across as a real bastard.

S Slow down. Talk slowly. (Did you ever try to yell slow?) Move slowly. Breathe slowly.

Some couples need to take control breaks even before the verbal argument stage. If there is a good deal of hurt and mistrust, you may need to take a break at the additional stressor stage. All of us know how to do that. We do not generally go off on judges, police officers, our bosses, etc. How do we do that? We talk ourselves out of it. You can do the same thing with your partner. Move the trike, get back in the car and talk yourself out of getting angry. The acronym we use for this technique is **SALT**.

S STOP. Say it out loud. To yourself. **STOP**. I don't want to become abusive over a tricycle.

A Air. Take some deep breaths. Let your system know you are not in danger. It can be helpful if you say the word, "calming", each time you inhale and if you smile when you exhale. (This works even if you don't feel like smiling.)

L List the alternatives. What other reason could there be for this to happen *besides* your partner just not caring about your feelings? Perhaps she broke her leg; maybe your child locked her in the closet; could be you won the lottery and she is so excited that she forgot to check the driveway; a spaceship could have abducted her. Remember, the purpose is *not* to find the real reason, but to break the chain of thought that can lead you into real trouble.

T Think about what you want. You want her to care more about you; enough so she is careful not to hurt your feelings. Do you really believe you'll get that by yelling and screaming at her? Think about it, we act as if the way to get our partners to be more caring with us is to make them feel like shit. Strange logic. What's the best way to get what you want?

Most couples could benefit from a control break at the very first stage of this cycle. When was the last time you and your partner went out together, without the kids, to do one of the fun things you used to do when you were dating? Have the two of you ever sat down and talked about how to arrange that first hour after you get home? That hour is known as the arsenic hour—the time you are most likely to fight or to poison the whole evening. If you look at how you spend your time, how much of it is spent in recreation? All of these examples are like investments in your relationship bank. They can help offset some of the withdrawals.

For he who gives no fuel to fire puts it out and likewise he who does not in the beginning nurse his wrath and does not puff himself up with anger takes precautions against it and destroys it.

Plutarch

A few preventative techniques for use only after you have cooled out. (You'll know you've cooled down when you no longer want to hurt your partner.)

1. Ask to hold her hand while you talk. It is much more difficult to get angry at someone you care about when you hold her hand. The process of doing that brings up some of the caring feelings that get submerged when you are angry.

2. Make your eyes soft. This not only shifts your mood, it is also a clear nonverbal message to her that you are not out for a fight.

3. Share a one-minute hug. Don't just grab her—she won't know what you're doing. Ask her for a hug. If she agrees, hold her for an entire minute. (Time it on your watch.) If you think about it, this is a very long hug. It doesn't even matter if she knows you are timing the hug. It works its magic just the same. At the end of the minute, both persons feel like someone pulled the plug and the stress drains out. It is a piece of magic caused by the release of endorphins—the brain's natural morphine—an anti-stress chemical. We recommend one-minute hugs each day, however, you should certainly try one before talking about something that upset you.

As we told you, all of the control break techniques work—if you try them. Find one that's comfortable for you, then make a commitment to using it. Choose to be in charge of your anger because you do not want it to destroy the things you value most.

An aggressor is not left unscathed, for it hurts to kill; it hurts to injure others; it hurts to scream and shout profane threats to another. Every time someone strikes another person in anger, hatred, or jealousy – whether impulsively or calculatedly – that someone loses something of himself. That person loses his control, loses his temper, loses his self-respect, loses the commendation of his friends and relatives, loses an opportunity to resolve the conflict (violence almost always compounds a problem, never simplifies it), and may even lose his freedom.

Violence is not a form of power but a negation of it. Violence does not achieve positive results and violence does not earn the respect and love of the partners or children in one's life. Rather, it alienates, it isolates, it obfuscates, it wears away a relationship. It produces fear, mistrust, hatred, pain, injury, sometimes death. It does not solidify a relationship; it blows it apart. Violence, then, is the poorest means to an end, if that end be a strong and loving partnership.

Violence is destructive to the self.

Man must evolve for all human conflict a method which rejects revenge, aggression and retaliation. The foundation of such a method is love.

Martin Luther King, Jr.

SECTION II
RESPECTFUL COMMUNICATION

RESPECTFUL COMMUNICATION

Many troubled couples cite lack of communication as the major problem in the relationship. Such a statement cannot be correct—not communicating is impossible. Whenever we are with another person we are communicating. At a minimum we are making statements about ourselves, about our perceptions and feelings toward the other person and about the relationship between us. Communication is a multi-level process on the parts of both the transmitter and the receiver. Compound this by the fact there is no common standard by which people are taught to communicate. Men and women tend to emphasize different levels. You can begin to see why opportunities for miscommunication abound.

In this segment of the book we attempt to give you some additional communication tools. We hope they will help you establish some clearer contacts *and* we offer them with some cautions:

1. Clarifying communications is an on-going process: no one ever really gets there.
2. Every interaction is different. What works today may not work tomorrow. What works with Person A may not be effective with Person B.
3. No one ever completely "hears" the message sent by another.

Given all this, you may be wondering why one should even bother to try. The fact that we are trying communicates caring and investment and is often enough to compensate for the other errors.

One more notion before we look at the nuts and bolts; it seems very important that we look at communication differences as differences, not as good versus bad or right versus wrong. We sometimes use this famous picture to help the men in our groups understand this idea.

Figure 7
COMMUNICATION DIFFERENCES

The picture on the following page is used to help you stay out of the "right-wrong" trap. What do you see when you look at the picture? Do you see an old woman? Or do you see a young woman?

If you see the old woman, cover her chin with your hand, imagine that her mouth is a necklace; her nose now becomes a jawbone, her left eye becomes an ear and the small bump under her right eye becomes a nose. Keep playing with it until you can also see the profile of a young woman.

If you see the young woman, reverse the sequence above so that her necklace becomes a mouth with very narrow lips, her ear becomes an eye and the white area below her necklace becomes a rather pointed chin. Keep playing with the picture until you can see the old woman.

Each person who looks at this picture sees one or the other first. Who sees it right? There really is no right or wrong: both pictures are there to be seen. The difference in emphasis on the ways to communicate is just like that. There is no right or wrong because both are there; both are valuable; both are effective ways to communicate.

So...there are two major traps involved in cross-gender communication. One is that neither person is aware that the other speaks in what is essentially a foreign language and the second is the tendency to classify differences as wrong. Avoiding these traps can take you a long way down the road to getting what you want in a relationship.

A different example is the curved mirror. Most of us have seen ourselves in a mirror that is intentionally curved; we look short and fat or tall and skinny or perhaps have a wave in the middle. What we may be less aware of is that each of us views the world through curved lenses.

The curves are caused by genetics, the family we are raised in, our social experiences and the culture in which we live. Each person's lens has unique curves, so no two people ever experience the same event in exactly the same way.

Sue grows up in a home where she often is hurt. She copes with the injuries by learning to withdraw inside herself and to build a wall to protect herself. She marries Paul, whose mother was not abusive, but was clinically depressed and not there for him emotionally. When Paul unintentionally says something that feels hurtful to Sue, she withdraws to protect herself.

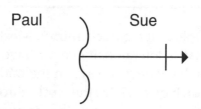

Paul experiences her withdrawal as abandonment, he is hurt and begins to sulk or pout. Who is right and who is wrong here? Each sees the situation right *from his point of view;* the error is caused by the bumps in the lenses. Unless each person understands that the other's point of view is different and legitimate, great fights can ensue.

As we talk about gender differences in communication, pay attention to how easy it is to slip into the "right/wrong" trap.

The first level we want to look at is the content level. The content of a communication is words we use. One type of content is called *concrete*—these are words from which a picture can be formed. The word "stud" is an example of concrete content. Concrete content communications are probably the simplest form; however, even these messages can be misunderstood as this joke may demonstrate.

> It seems these two ministers died and went to heaven. When they arrived, St. Peter welcomed them and explained that he knew they were going to be happy there. There was however, one small glitch: the contractors had somehow fallen behind and the new arrivals' condos were not quite ready yet. St. Peter then explained that he wanted to send the ministers back to earth for a few weeks until their new homes were ready. Each minister would be allowed to go back to earth in any form he chose. One of the ministers quickly spoke up and explained that he had always wanted to be an eagle soaring over the Grand Canyon. St. Peter said "fine" and sent

him on his way. The other minister then explained that he had always wanted to be a "real cool stud." St. Peter again said "fine" and sent him back to earth. After a few weeks, St. Peter called one of the angels and asked him to go retrieve the two ministers. When he was asked where to find them, he replied that one of them was flying over the Grand Canyon. "The other one may be a little harder to find. He's somewhere on a snow tire in Buffalo."

Now we suspect that the picture of a "real cool stud" that the minister had in his head was pretty different from the one St. Peter came up with. Fixing this level of miscommunication is relatively easy...if we have enough words around any given concrete word, we easily change the pictures in our heads until they match. If St. Peter had thought to ask "What kind of a 'real cool stud?', the minister would have very different memories of his visit back to earth.

Another type of content is *abstract words*—words you cannot compare with pictures. One example of an abstract word is "commitment." Two people can have a conversation about commitment even though neither one has a picture of what commitment is. Because we have no easy way to compare, we tend to assume that our conversation partner understands the concept the same way we do. This assumption is often dead wrong and can cause major arguments.

We chose the word "commitment" as our example because it is a word that we stumbled over in the early days of our relationship. Whenever Margy would mention commitment, Denny would turn pale, start to shake and begin to lace up his track shoes. Margy found this to be a rather bizarre reaction. Over time we found that for Denny, commitment meant an external promise that locked you in forever—the trap doors closing. For Margy, commitment is an internal process that governs her behavior and may be reassessed in response to the reactions of others—no trap here. Couples often have major battles over abstract words; rarely do they sit down to decipher what the word means to each of them.

Another level of communication is the *feelings* level. In every contact we communicate something of our feelings about ourselves, our feelings about the other person, and our feelings about the relationship between us. The most common ways of expressing feelings are verbally (we put into words what we are feeling), nonverbally (through tones, attitudes, body language, etc.) and by our behaviors or what we choose to do.

The verbal expression of feelings is fraught with opportunities for miscommunication. First, some of us are not very good at figuring out *what* we feel. Then, we may not be able to easily put the feeling into words. Sometimes, we feel more than one thing or even have conflicting feelings present at the same time. To make matters worse, the speaker's definition of a feeling may not match that of the listener. For example, "upset" may mean "agitated and excited" to you but "anxious and frightened" to your partner.

Then one has to interpret what level or intensity of feeling is being expressed. If someone says he is "enraged," it is easy to see he is not talking about a minor irritation. Interpreting "hurt," however, is much more difficult. If someone scratches your arm, you might say he "hurt" you; if your partner sleeps with your best friend, you might say she "hurt" you. Same word—*very* different levels of feeling.

You can share with your partner that certain names used during a fight "hurt" you—she may hear that you were scratched, when, in reality, you are trying to convey a much deeper injury. Should she repeat this behavior next time, you can easily feel not only injured but betrayed— and your subsequent anger can escalate big time.

Nonverbal communication has some special problems over and above the ones we've already talked about. We learn nonverbal communication nonverbally, so we tend to experience our way as the *way things are*, rather than as something we learned. If your parents taught you that the digits on your hands are called "wompas," it would not take you long to learn that everyone else calls them "fingers." You would likely decide that you had been taught the wrong word.

Sometimes different names for the same thing are regional. Margy grew up in Montana where the storage departments in the dashboards of cars are called "jockey-boxes." When she moved to the midwest she quickly learned to switch to "glove compartments" (being laughed at is a powerful inducement to change).

Learning the right word, or a different word, is relatively easy. We make those adjustments throughout our lives. Nonverbal re-learning is *much* more difficult; generally because we blame the other person for the error and see no need to change our part of the interaction.

One powerful type of nonverbal behavior is an entire set of rules about our "personal space." Each of us has a personal space that he carries around with him. This space does not start at our skin but instead extends like a bubble around us. When two people talk, they generally arrange themselves so that the distance between them honors both personal spaces. If someone violates this rule, and steps into your personal space, you will react by holding your breath and tightening up until you see what his intention is.

It appears that everyone has a personal space. However, the area that is experienced as one's personal space varies from country to country. In America, personal space is about one arm's length—this assumes a normal situation. One's personal space increases when he is angry. A person may then need a much greater space in order not to feel intruded upon. Sometimes an angry person feels that his partner "gets right up in his face" even though she is, in reality, honoring his normal personal space.

Personal spaces in England are larger. Two Englishmen talking will stand 3-4 paces further apart than will two Americans. When an American talks to an Englishman, the Englishman keeps backing up and the American keeps moving in. Because each feels his own experience of *personal space* is the way it's supposed to be, the Englishman blames American for "pushiness" and the American sees the Englishman as "cold and unfriendly."

Italians, on the other hand, have smaller personal spaces. Two Italians talking will stand so close they are almost touching. Italians who talk to Americans find them rigid and unfriendly...Americans find Italians "pushy." We suspect that Italians and Englishmen can only talk on the phone. It is hard to imagine how they could manage the difference in comfortable distance.

Personal space rules and the strategies for dealing with rule violations are very powerful. A good example of this is elevator behavior. Everyone knows how to behave on an elevator. You can stand with your back to any of the three walls, but not the door. If the elevator is crowded, you are to be still and quiet. Everyone spreads out as much as possible the minute anyone gets off. All of these behaviors are *nonverbal* messages which tell others you're aware that you are in their space; that you intend no harm and you'll get out of their space as soon as possible.

If you don't believe these rules are powerful, try breaking one. Face the crowd, instead of the door. Or better yet, the next time you're standing next to someone, don't move when others get off. You will create some very nervous people.

If you wish to try breaking a nonverbal rule that is a little less intimidating, the next time you're with someone at one of the fast-food restaurants which has the little tables for two, violate the rule which says that each of you "owns" half of the table. As you talk, gradually begin moving some of your things onto "his" side of the table. It can make for a very dicey lunch!

Where did you learn all of the nonverbal lessons? From your parents. Once you grew beyond the infant stage, your parents' nonverbal messages (to which children are *very* sensitive) "taught" you the correct distance to stand, etc. Even very young children rarely make nonverbal mistakes.

We also learn to "read" some of our partner's nonverbal language. If you live with someone, you can become quite adept at sensing her mood, even when she does not speak. Unfortunately, our ability to read other "channels" is not so well developed. There are areas where the bumps in our lenses cause major errors. Distortions caused by gender socializations are particularly pronounced. We misread not only subtle messages, we sometimes experience the meaning as *opposite* of what was intended. Our misunderstandings (and being misunderstood) are so rampant that many authors talk of this phenomenon in terms of separate languages for men and women.

The analogy we use is to compare the many channels of communication to several different radios playing but tuned to separate stations. Each person is capable of attending to any of the stations; however, men and women are socialized to listen to different ones. No one can actively attend to all the channels at the same time. No one's choice of which one to listen to is wrong or better than someone else's choice. Neither men nor women "do it right." If we can step out of the "blame trap" and learn to explore the differences, we not only come closer to really hearing our partners (and being heard), we can also get a view of a very different world.

The process of learning to communicate can bring real intimacy and is fascinating and fun to boot! If you find yourself judging your partner's ways as wrong or inferior, just remember that these are skills you also possess—housed in parts of you that were not allowed to develop. Where communication is concerned, each of us is born ambidextrous; we are poorer because one hand is bound up by social restrictions.

A man's world is organized around competition. He is judged all his life by how well he compares to other men in terms of accomplishments. Men are taught to value the parts of themselves that strive for autonomy and independence. There are rules governing "fair play" in their endless *winner-loser* games; however, winning is more important than being fair. The NFL, for example, has recently stopped using instant replay—it is okay to win by playing unfair if you don't get caught. Men are expected to do things well, including their jobs, sports, house and car maintenance. Problem-solving, fixing it, getting the job done are the end goals. Communicating is often seen only as a means to accomplishing the task.

A woman's world is organized around connecting. A woman is judged all her life by how well she forms and maintains relationships. Women are taught to value the parts of themselves that strive for closeness and joining. They also have rules for "fair play" in their cooperative games, however being included is more important than being fair. Many a girl has been "snubbed" by her best friend when she lost favor with the "in" crowd. Women are expected to do all the relationship maintenance tasks. Communicating is often seen as the means to establishing and maintaining the connections.

Both worlds are terrible, and wonderful. We need both accomplishment and connection. What is tragic is not the differences, but that no one tells us there are two separate worlds. Actually each of us inhabits a separate, unique world—a story for another book. Being so unaware, we struggle to make our partners fit in our own world, unable to make sense of their behavior. Our failure leaves us frustrated and angry, leads to blame, often causes disrupted relationships and sometimes evokes violence. Let's look at some common examples.

He works all day at a job he does not like. He takes all the overtime he can get. He's working to provide for his family. This is his way of showing them how much he cares. Ask her if he cares and she is likely to say "Hell no. He's married to the job".

She wants to connect with him when he comes home from work. She asks, "How was your day?", meaning, connect with me by sharing a feeling. He has no new information to give her, so he replies, "It was okay". She gets angry and upset at what feels like an unwillingness to connect to her. She may complain that he never talks to her or that he never tells her a damned thing. He feels like he truthfully replied and has no idea why she is upset.

When he calls a buddy he says, "You want to go fishing Saturday? Great. I'll pick you up at 8:00. You pick up the beer." He hangs up the phone, having efficiently accomplished the task of setting up the get-together. The connection to his buddy will be strengthened by *doing* something together.

On the other hand, she talks to her girlfriend for an hour and a half, and may call the same woman to talk more after dinner. He can't imagine what they could have to talk about, and if he eavesdrops, he may go away disgusted since they are talking about "nothing". The women are talking to connect. They both know the content is not important. Women sometime think men have no friends because "You guys never talk about anything".

He needs new tires for the car. It's not likely he'll take his buddy with him. If he did, he couldn't imagine that the two of them could shop for tires all afternoon, not find what they want, and report that they had a good time. She can, and does, go with a friend to the mall shopping for a new blouse. She looks at 500 blouses without finding one she likes, stays gone all afternoon, and reports that they had a great time. He goes to do the job. She goes to make a connection. Both feel good if they accomplish what they set out to do.

Did you ever go out to eat with another couple? If either of the men had to go to the bathroom, he *certainly* did not ask the other guy to go with him. The women, on the other hand, pass an invisible signal between them, stand up in unison and head for the restroom. Sometimes one of them doesn't have to go to the bathroom, in fact, at times the one who initiated the visit forgets she wanted to go and neither one uses the facilities! Again, men go to do the job and they certainly don't want or need any help. Women go to talk without the guys; using the bathroom is incidental.

He never wants to look "one down", so he attempts to solve any problems in his head before he talks about them. She expects to solve problems together. She feels ordered around and left out when he produces the solution. He feels confused and overwhelmed by all the conflicting feelings and thoughts she expresses during her problem-solving process.

He starts to get too angry and shuts down or attempts to leave in order to cool out. He's expressing his care and concern for her. He doesn't want to get so angry he hurts her. She experiences either action as his breaking the connection, meaning he *doesn't* care. She may respond by moving closer in an attempt to stay connected—a move he experiences as her "getting right up in my face". He may may even interpret such moves as her "wanting to be hit".

He's likely to feel that **fairness** would dictate the two of you take turns at making minor **decisions** like where to go for dinner. She believes that both your feelings **need** to be considered, so the connections stay solid. He asks her where she wants to go for dinner, meaning it's your turn to decide. She replies that she doesn't care, meaning I have no strong preference. How do you feel? He takes the decision back and takes her somewhere. She's angry and feels like he never cares about where she wants to eat. If she tells him this, he thinks he asked her, for crying out loud. What does she want, anyway?

The list could go on and on. you can dissect virtually any disagreement you have had and find that the difficulty lies at the interface between the two worlds.

The examples we've chosen are, for the most part, humorous. The down side to all this is that these basic misunderstandings can lead two people, each of whom is demonstrating his caring as best he knows, to a divorce court where each feels that the other doesn't care at all.

How do we use this new information? In general, the strategy is to stop the process when differences come up and work toward understanding the meanings for each of you. We have gathered a few specific tools that may be helpful.

> ## If you are losing a tug-o-war
> ## with a tiger,
> ## Give him the rope before
> ## he gets to your arm.
> ## You can always buy a new rope.
>
> Max Gunther

TALKING TO HER WHEN YOU'RE ANGRY

Rule # 1—Don't

Cool out first. Trying to talk to someone when you are angry is like trying to change a flat tire without jacking the car up first. It may be possible, but it's a very tough job.

Rule # 2—Don't Put Her on the Defensive

This is not gender specific. Human beings appear to have some built-in software that leads us to withdraw or to attack when we feel attacked.

Either stance dooms communication efforts. There is no guaranteed way to prevent defensiveness but there are some techniques that greatly improve your chances.

First, watch your words. Some words pull for defensiveness all by themselves, regardless of your intent. Some examples follow.

WHY?—The Linguistic Fundamental Attribution Error

Say what? That one zipped right over your head? Not surprising. Those fancy words are familiar to only a small group of specialists (social psychologists) who study the ways people decide why something happens. An attribution is, basically, the cause one decides on. For example, I recently skidded my car into a ditch. I attributed the accident to the ice on the road. These scientists have discovered that people make a common error when they make attributions. It is an error so common that it's called fundamental. The error is, that when we see someone doing something, we are likely to give more weight to his character (that's the way he is) than to the situation when we decide on the cause.

Denny's desk is a good example. It is currently a mess, piled high with stacks of papers and unsorted junk. Margy is likely to tell you that it is that way because Denny is messy and unorganized. The reality is that, overall, Denny is quite neat and organized. One of the ways the specialists have for determining that we make this mistake is the fact that if you look at Margy's desk (which is also a mess) and ask her why, she is likely to tell you that she haven't been feeling well, have been swamped at work, etc.

It's not important that you know about or understand fundamental attribution errors. You can make a big difference by changing one word—WHY to three other words, WHAT HAPPENED THAT. When we ask "why?", there is an implied criticism of our partner's character. She is likely to become defensive which is a lead-in to a fight. When we ask "what happened that?", we imply that there could be a good reason and that we are not blaming. Try it, you'll be pleasantly surprised at the result. This is also a great self esteem builder to use with the kids. "Why were you late" is a very different question than "What happened that you were late?".

BUT—The Great Negator
- I appreciate your tidying up *but*
- I love you *but*
- I don't want to hurt you *but*
- You did a great job *but*

Notice what happens to your stomach when you hear the word "but"? It's amazing how one little word can wipe out all that came before it as we wait for the zinger to follow. Change your "buts" to "ands" to make a big difference.

- I appreciate your tidying up *and* I would prefer to arrange my tools myself.
- I love you *and* we need to spend some time talking about our problems.
- I don't want to hurt you *and* I need to talk about something that is difficult for you to hear.
- You did a great job *and* I want to show you how I like the clothes folded.

ALWAYS–NEVER

These buzz-bombs virtually guarantee to set off defensiveness since no one always or never does anything. When used, they imply something about the person's character. They are experienced as fault-finding (exceptions are apparently not taken into account) and they dredge up the past instead of dealing only with the current issue. Eliminate them altogether.

MUST–SHOULD

These are words that shift the discussion from the problem to a question of who has the right to be in charge. A power struggle then ensues. It is not possible to win a power struggle in a relationship; even if the decision is awarded to you the relationship loses.

ANGRY

Research shows that the word "angry" implies angry *at* and your listener will assume that the target is her. Use *upset* instead. Upset also has the effect of pulling up some of the other things you are probably feeling, like hurt, fear, etc.

"I" Statements

Another way to minimize defensiveness is to use "I" statements. When you use "I" statements you talk about yourself, not the other person. "I" statements not only reduce defensiveness, they increase your power by keeping the spotlight on you, and they remove the biggest counterargument. If I say, "You are rude and lazy", you can easily reply that you are not and then we can fight about it. If I say, "I am upset because you forgot to set the trash out", you cannot say "You are not" without feeling foolish. "I" statements begin with "I". The next word should be *am* or *was* followed by a feeling. If you say "I feel that", you are likely to come our with a thought instead.

Sharing a feeling is important to the connection process in *her* world. Then you can say *because* and describe what upset you using camera talk.

Camera talk describes *only* what a camera would see. For example, "I am upset because my supervisor stopped in with me after work and the living room was a mess." The camera could see that the living room was a mess. "I am upset because you didn't get off your ass and clean the living room." is *not* camera talk because the camera could not see that.

Notice that there is a period at the end of the "I" statement. It means to *stop talking*. Men often piss their power away by rambling on about every unresolved issue in the relationship. Stop. *Do not tell her the solution.* You did not marry a stupid woman.

Give her chance to respond. If she doesn't, *then* ask her for what you want, taking care not to slip in an attack. She, of course, is entitled to say "no". At any point the two of you can problem-solve to come up with a different solution. This technique is relatively easy and effective—*provided* that you cool out first.

CHOICES FOR DEALING
WITH YOUR PARTNER'S ANGER

There are three basic ways to deal with your partner when she is angry. You can choose to:

- get angry in return
- refuse to interact with her until she cools down
- help her cool down

A man typically makes one of three major strategic errors when his partner is angry—he feels attacked and retaliates, he tries to fix the problem that caused the anger, or he gives up and withdraws. His partner experiences the retaliation as a sign to escalate, his attempts to fix the problem as him not understanding, and the withdrawal as a sign he doesn't care. Given her reactions, it is easy to understand why none of these tactics work.

The most effective way to help your partner cool down is to *listen to HER*, not to her *words* but to her *feelings. When your partner is angry with you, she feels like you hurt her.* For her, that pain is like a truck parked on her foot. Until it is moved, nothing else matters.

Let's look at the consequences of each of these choices:

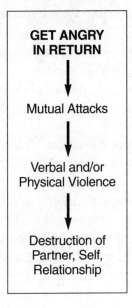
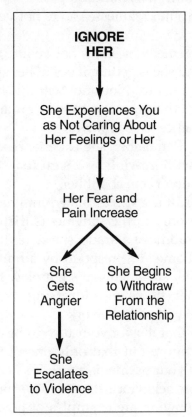
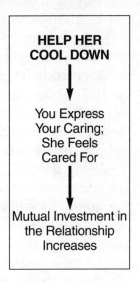

"Oh sure", you're saying to yourself. "Fat chance". "I've tried that before and things have only gotten worse." "You don't know my partner, there's no chance of calming her down." We did not say this would be easy. However, it is possible and is well worth the effort it takes.

The specific way to address that pain is to borrow the iceberg model we talked about at the beginning of Section I. First, acknowledge that you see she is angry, then tell her you understand she feels hurt by what you did and finally, assure her you did not intend to hurt her and that you care about her.

Some Things to Think About

- When you see a red flag, it means *STOP* not *CHARGE*.
- Even when her anger seems irrational to you, your best bet is to listen.
- Remember, she is not willing to listen to you at the moment.

- Be glad she's not bottling up her anger so it comes out in other ways that undermine the relationship.
- Learn to expect some craziness. You're not very sane when you're angry, either.
- When she yells, remember she is not yelling at you, she is yelling for herself. Be glad she is getting it out of her system.
- Take some deep breaths. Not only will this help you stay cool, it will send a nonverbal message to her you are not escalating and will give her a chance to cool down.
- Try to stay open. Remember, she experiences your shutting down, being quiet, or withdrawing as a sign that you are breaking the connections and don't care about her.
- Ignore the bullets. If she has escalated into name-calling and accusations, respond only to the statements that are camera-talk. For example, in the middle of a tirade, she states that you forgot to pick up milk on the home. You respond by admitting that is true and ignore all the other statements. It's not okay for you to take abuse from your partner; however addressing that when she is in the middle of an angry fit will not work.
- Remind yourself that it's not your turn to be crazy. Successful couples manage to figure out that only one of you is allowed to be crazy at a time. If your partner is angry, it's her turn.

Understand that her behavior is largely determined by what she has been through. The following are examples of how this understanding can help you. If you were parked at a red light, and a car rear-ended you, you might get out and go back to yell at the driver. Would you still be angry at him if you discovered that a truck behind him hadn't stopped and pushed him into you? Or, imagine you are a counselor in a residential program for children who have been abandoned, rejected and generally kicked around by the people in their lives. One of the young teens comes into your office and starts yelling at you, cursing and shouting about how much he hates you. Would you respond with anger and set up punishment for him if you knew he had gone to court that day to discover his parents had surrendered custody of him, that they had given him to the welfare department?

A Note About Defending Yourself—Don't

This is the most difficult aspect of helping your partner cool down. Our natural tendency when feeling attacked is to defend ourselves, either by retaliation or withdrawal. Defending yourself is always a mistake. First of all, your partner's attack is caused by her pain and fear—*not* by you. Defending yourself reinforces her erroneous belief that you are the cause. In addition, defending yourself is an admission that at least part of what is being said is true.

There is a crude bar joke that illustrates this last point. A woman was sitting in a bar when a man came up and asked her if she would sleep with him for a million dollars. She hesitated only a short time before she agreed that she would do that. He then asked her if she would sleep with him for five dollars. She became very indignant and said, "No, what kind of girl do you take me for, anyway?" He then replied "We've already established what kind of girl you are; we're just haggling about the price."

Arguing about how much of her accusation is true only puts you in that girl's position and ignores the real issue, which is your partner's pain and fear. This is one of the reasons that arguments don't get resolved. The two of you end up arguing over what kind of driver you are instead of moving the truck off her foot.

There is a powerful technique you can use to manage your feeling of being attacked—SHIFT INTO NEUTRAL GEAR. You can do this by making neutral statements that do not address right/wrong, agreement/disagreement, or good/bad. Examples of such statements are, "I understand that's how you feel right now" and "That's one way to look at it".

This is not a tool that is intended to help her cool down, it is intended to give you an option other than defending yourself. However, often one of the side-effects when you don't defend yourself is a reduction in the anger level on her part.

NON-NEGOTIABLE ITEMS

The navy was holding a training exercise. It was a foggy night, so the captain of the ship was on the bridge. A look-out reported a light off the starboard bow. Since it was not moving, it was apparent that the two ships were on a collision course. The captain ordered a signal sent, instructing the other vessel to change course 20 degrees. A return signal advised him to change course 20 degrees.

"Signal him that I am an admiral. *He* should change course 20 degrees."

The return signal was "I am a seaman 2nd class. Advise you turn course 20 degrees".

By now the admiral was hot and fired off, "I am a battleship. Turn 20 degrees".

The reply came back, "I am a lighthouse".

Each person has such items, issues on which he or she will not compromise. Most non-negotiable items surface during dating.For example, if you believe that a mother should stay home with the children and you intend for your future wife to do that, it is not likely that you will continue to date a girl when you find out she plans a career. Or, if you believe you will look silly if your wife were taller than you, you would be unlikely to ask a taller girl for a date.

Other non-negotiable items are agreed upon before marriage such as, your belief that the children should not be spanked, extended family members should be allowed to live with you if they need a place, or that your wife should let you handle her paycheck. Such items are generally discussed and an agreement reached before the circumstances come up.

The non-negotiable items that surface ahead of time do not generally cause the difficulties that the unknown non-negotiable items do. There are several reasons why the unknown non-negotiables cause so much trouble. Couples get lulled into a false belief that they have negotiated all of the major hurdles before they get married. Marriage involves a great deal of negotiating—the non-negotiable items get lost in the crowd. Couples sometime feel that the marriage license gives each of them permission to change the other. There is no common agreement about which issues are non-negotiable; what cannot be negotiated by one person seems very open to compromise to the partner.

How to Recognize an Unknown Non-negotiable Issue

Look for issues that the two of you have argued about time and again with no progress and the only change being an increasing sense of frustration. It's likely the issue is non-negotiable for one of you.

Non-negotiable issues are idiosyncratic, that is, they are different for each person. Items become non-negotiable because of a person's past experience. Therefore, one person cannot decide what should be non-negotiable for another.

These issues are not necessarily non-negotiable over time. An issue that is non-negotiable at age 25 may seem relatively unimportant at age 40. Other items may remain non-negotiable for a lifetime, such as one's religious faith.

Because of the pre-selection process, most non-negotiable items are not that way for both partners. If such is the case, there are basically three ways to handle the dilemma:

- the couple splits up
- an agreement to disagree is reached, if possible
- one or both partners seek counseling.

Issues are generally non-negotiable because they threaten one of two major processes—integrity, i.e., a person's sense of who he is, or freedom. Healthy people will not willingly give up either of these. An integrity example that often causes on-going friction is your relationship to your friends. Men who have grown up with a particular group of buddies may experience those friends as a part of themselves. Wives may not understand that facet of the relationship and view old friends as a part of your life to be given up when you get married. She doesn't know that the issue is non-negotiable, *since she feels it should be negotiable*, and she continues to attempt to persuade you to stop seeing your friends.

An example of disguised freedom issue is what may look like the battle over housework. Wives, particularly those with young children, have *very little* freedom. (Note: here freedom is defined as that time when a person can do whatever he wants to do, without feeling guilty.) Small children may limit a woman's freedom to a few minutes here and there during the day. She may choose to exercise her very limited freedom by choosing when or if she will do the housework. You come home to a messy house, do not understand the submerged freedom issue, and blow up because she didn't do her job that day.

Dealing With Non-negotiable Items

Get them out in the open by discussing not only the issue but the underlying facets which make it non-negotiable. Be aware that continued attempts to change non-negotiable items result in anger, bitterness, and frustration.

Remember that no matter how easy the desired change may look to you, if it is non-negotiable for your partner, she *cannot* change it. *That lighthouse ain't movin'*. Ask yourself if this is a bottom-line issue for you—are you willing to split up over this item? If not, back off. You don't have to like it but you do need to be able to accept it as a part of your partner.

HOW TO COMMUNICATE TO RESOLVE DIFFERENCES

Fights over differences don't begin with the first word spoken, they start in an atmosphere created by the angry partner. Remember, differences are not an issue of right or wrong, just different. The real issue is not who wins, but how we can find a solution that fits for both of us.

The differences between you do not have the power to destroy your relationship; however, the process by which you resolve those differences does.

Learning to use the Differences Decision Tree that follows is like learning to drive a car—there are many parts, each is important, and managing all of them seems impossible. Each of us struggled through that feeling of being overwhelmed because our desire to be able to drive was even stronger than our sense of not being able to manage. You can do the same with this process. Sometimes you will over-steer, sometimes you won't regulate the speed just right, and you may even run right off the road! Keep practicing. In time, the process will come to feel natural and automatic.

Figure 8
DIFFERENCES DECISION TREE

DECISION POINT #1—Am I cooled out?

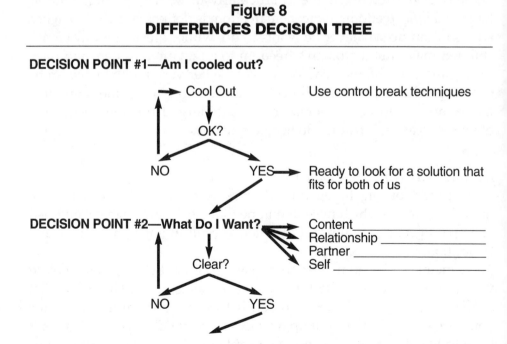

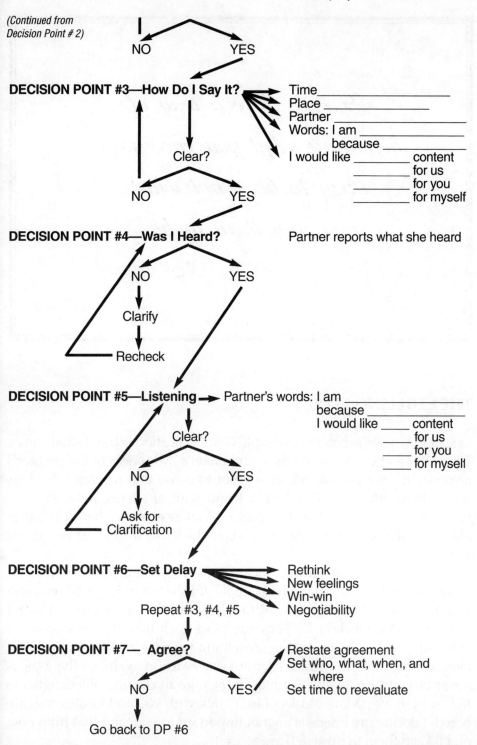

(Continued from Decision Point # 2)

NO   YES

DECISION POINT #3—How Do I Say It?

Time_____
Place _____
Partner _____
Words: I am _____
        because _____
I would like _____ content
            _____ for us
            _____ for you
            _____ for myself

Clear?

NO   YES

DECISION POINT #4—Was I Heard?   Partner reports what she heard

NO   YES

Clarify

Recheck

DECISION POINT #5—Listening → Partner's words: I am _____
        because _____
I would like ____ content
            ____ for us
            ____ for you
            ____ for myself

Clear?

NO   YES

Ask for Clarification

DECISION POINT #6—Set Delay

Rethink
New feelings
Win-win
Negotiability

Repeat #3, #4, #5

DECISION POINT #7— Agree?

Restate agreement
Set who, what, when, and
        where
Set time to reevaluate

NO   YES

Go back to DP #6

> *"People have a way of*
> *becoming what you encourage*
> *them to be – not what*
> *you nag them to be."*
>
> *S. N. Parker*

THE CHILLING EFFECT

One of the major problems in couple communication is the chilling effect. The chilling effect is caused by each person's awareness of his partner's response to sharing, and his desire not to cause that response. In time, the chilling effect can build up a frigid wall of silence between you. Sometimes the wall is blasted apart by violence; most often it is left in place and added to over time until it is so thick that the two of you are no longer connected.

Our intentions for adding blocks of ice are generally good—unfortunately, the end result is not. For example, if I share a feeling with you and you get upset, I may decide not to talk about that anymore so I won't hurt you. (One block of ice goes into place each time it comes up and I don't share.) If you are sharing something with me and I get angry and blow up, you may be afraid to cause that reaction again, so the topic is never brought up again. You may, in fact, go to considerable lengths to hide it from me. (More blocks of ice.) I talk with you and I notice you are bored. I decide my interests are not important to you, and that from now on I'll keep them to myself. (Ice, ice, ice.)

Figure 9
THE CHILLING EFFECT

Thawing the wall must be a slow, gentle process. The ice protects each of you from feeling many hurts and fears.

REMINDERS

Never will I see a castle

And not think of you. . .

Wondering what might have been

Had we built the walls around us

Instead of between us.

Royce Ellis Daniels

Guidelines

Start by talking about your awareness of the existence of the wall and how you feel about it being there. Remember, this is not a fault-finding mission.

Make an effort to stop adding blocks on your side. *Before* sharing something with her talk about your fear that she will be angry, upset, or bored. Tell her that it is not your intention to cause that feeling. Ask her is there is another way for you to talk about it. Ask her if she wants to hear. If she says "No", respect her wishes. Share with her your sadness at adding another block between you.

Own up to the times that your reactions have caused the chilling effect. Ask her to try again. Assure her that you are working to control your reactions so it is always safe for her to share with you.

There is a very delicate balance between taking care of oneself and being aware of one's impact on his partner. The fact that we do not achieve this balance most of the time is not important. The fact that we try is important.

HOW TO ASK FOR CHANGES

Another area in which it is easy to make a mistake is the times when we want to ask our partner to change some particular behavior. Many people ask in such a way that they unknowingly set up a power struggle. Such interchanges usually go like this:

> Dave picks a time when he and Susan are not fighting. He is not angry and uses "I" statements. He says, "Honey, I am really bothered when I get a drink before bed and find the dinner dishes are still in the sink. I would appreciate it if you would do them after dinner."
>
> Susan then says, "OK". She actually does the dishes after dinner for two or three nights and on the third night she is back to her old routine.
>
> Dave feels hurt because she is not considering his feelings and gets angry at what he sees as her inconsiderateness and/or laziness.
>
> What neither person may realize is that Dave set up a power struggle when he asked Susan to change her behavior. This is how it happened. When Dave stated how he felt, he implicitly said "These are my feelings. If you care about me, you will put your own feelings aside and accommodate me with this request". She agreed to do as he asked, but after a day or two, she began to become angry at the implicit put-down of her feelings and decided her feelings count as much as his do.

Preventing this type of power struggle is easy. After stating your feelings and what you would like, ask her is she is willing to do that. The process of asking her implies that her feelings are as important as yours. The risk, of course, is that she will say "no". The process of asking gives her the right to do that. If she says no, then the two of you can negotiate. This process nurtures a relationship, rather than leaving both of you with the destruction caused by power struggles in intimate relationships.

To laugh is to risk appearing the fool.

To weep is to risk appearing sentimental.

To reach out is to risk involvement.

To expose feelings is to risk exposing your true self.

*To place your ideas and dreams before the crowd is to risk
their love.*

To love is to risk not being loved in return.

To live is to risk dying.

To hope is to risk despair.

To try is to risk failure.

But the greatest hazard in life is to risk nothing.

*The one who risks nothing does nothing and has nothing
– and finally is nothing.*

He may avoid suffering and sorrow,

But he simply cannot learn, feel, change, grow or love.

*Chained by his certitude, he is a slave; he has forfeited
freedom.*

Only one who risks is free!

Anonymous

ACTIVE LISTENING

Active listening is one of the most important techniques that we teach the men who participate in our groups. Many of them report this tool is the most powerful one they learn to use.

Active listening is not sitting there, nodding, and saying nothing. It is not half of a conversation. Active listening is a specialized skill that can greatly increase the intimacy level in your relationship. Listening increases understanding and builds empathy, the ability to put yourself in your partner's shoes. How do you do it?

- Pay attention. It is not possible to listen and do anything else at the the same time.
- Respond to the feeling being expressed rather than the content.
- Have a curious attitude. You are interested in what the topic *means* to your partner, not the topic itself.
- Reflect back to her what you think you've heard. If you don't have it right, she has a chance to correct you.
- Don't give any advice. This is not a problem-solving session.
- Do not put your stuff out there. This makes it a conversation instead of listening.
- If you do talk about your reactions, use them as a means of turning the topic back to her. For example, "I would be really frustrated if that happened to me. Is that how it feels to you?"

A few minutes of active listening every day can be powerful glue. Studies indicate that couples who have been together for awhile listen to each other only about ten minutes a week. No wonder they grow apart!

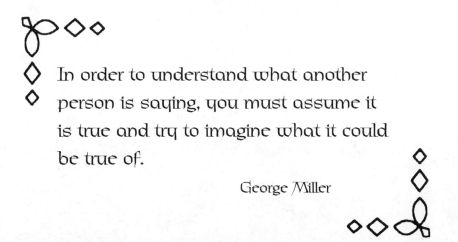

In order to understand what another person is saying, you must assume it is true and try to imagine what it could be true of.

George Miller

Section III
Dealing With Special Challenges

Each of the issues discussed in this section deserves a book of its own. Many such books are available and most of these issues also have specialized treatments and help available. The mini-segments in this section do not reflect the severity of these problems, nor do we pretend that one or two pages of information can begin to treat them. This section is only intended to highlight some of the issues for which the two of you may need to get help.

ALCOHOLISM/DRUG ABUSE & DOMESTIC VIOLENCE

Alcoholism and/or drug abuse does not cause domestic violence. Although 60% to 80% of arrests for domestic violence also involve drinking or drug use by one or both parties, 75% of all fights that become violent involve no drug or alcohol abuse. Some professionals believe that "stuffers" sometime drink *in order* to become violent. Afterwards, such a person can say that he didn't really mean it, it only happened because he was drinking.

Why talk about it at all then? Discussing the problem in a book devoted to helping men stop the abuse in their relationships is important because the choice of using drugs and/or alcohol to solve one's problems or to stop one's pain is choosing not to grow. Without that growth, one cannot make better choices. Choosing not to deal with an alcohol or drug problem literally means choosing to die alone.

> The answer doesn't lie in learning
> to protect ourselves from life –
> it lies in learning how to become strong enough
> to let a bit more of it in.
>
> *Merle Shain*

If you are saying to yourself, "I don't have a problem, I can quit any-time" or "I don't have a problem, I only drink on weekends" or *any* state-ment that begins with "I don't have a problem..." you should be aware that one of the principal symptoms of chemical dependency is denial. Ask yourself the following questions:

1. Have I ever felt like I should cut down on my drinking?
2. Do I get annoyed when someone talks to me about my drinking?
3. Do I ever feel guilty about my drinking?

If the answer to any one of these questions is "yes", you may indeed have a problem.

The alcoholic/drug abuser not only denies that he has a problem, he also denies that his problem affects his relationship or his family. If you believe this, you owe it to your family to attend an ACOA meeting. ACOA stands for Adult Children of Alcoholics. You can hear first-hand, the pain and fear that is experienced by your children. You may also become aware of the rage these adults feel as they grapple with the dam-age that such a childhood caused and continues to cause in their lives.

One of the analogies used to talk about life with an alcoholic parent is that it is like having a rhinoceros in your living room. The non-abusing parent covers it with a tablecloth and everyone pretends that it is a table. Of course someone, usually the partner, has to clean up the shit he or she leaves all over. Occasionally he or she goes on a rampage destroying things and trampling everyone in sight. Afterwards the family members clean up as best they can, the other parent puts the tablecloth back on and everyone pretends there is no rhinoceros and no one is afraid.

If you have a drug/alcohol problem it is nearly always the primary problem. That means you cannot work on any other problem until you begin to recover. Recovery is not a solitary process—you cannot do it alone. You may be able to stop drinking or drugging alone; however, you then become a "dry drunk", maintaining all of the destructive character-istics. A rhinoceros who stops going on rampages is still a rhinoceros.

Remember, choosing not to go into recovery is choosing to die alone.

If you are married to an alcohol or drug abuser *run*, don't walk, to an ALANON meeting. She has chosen to destroy herself. Your attempts to save her, to change her, or to relate to her are not only fruitless, they are likely to make things worse. ALANON can teach you what is possible, and what is not. You can then make good choices—for her, for your fami-ly, and for yourself.

Security is mostly a superstition.
It does not exist in nature,
nor do the children of men as a whole experience it.
Avoidance of danger is no safer
in the long run than outright exposure.
Life is either a daring adventure, or nothing.

Helen Keller
The Open Door 1902

JEALOUSY

Jealousy, like anger, is a misunderstood emotion fueled by feelings kept below the surface.

The jealous person experiences this jealousy as caused by his partner's behavior. This is a major distortion since that feeling is really fueled by the underlying fear of loss. That fear, in turn, is driven by shame.

Shame is a very deep, very primitive feeling that there is something wrong with me, that I am not lovable, that my partner would not care about me if he really knows who I am. Shame comes from poor parenting and usually cannot be overcome without professional counseling. Experiencing shame is very painful—the fear of losing someone you love is very frightening. It is easier not to experience those feelings and to blame one's partner for causing the jealousy.

The partner of a jealous person finds himself driven away from the person he loves by her ownership behavior. What he experiences is his partner's attempts to hang on to him by owning him—and not the underlying fear of loss. No one responds well to feeling like someone wants to own him; most people respond by instinctively pulling back. When the jealous person senses this withdrawal, her fear of loss increases. This then causes her jealous ownership behaviors to increase. This drives the partner even further away. The very process by which the person attempts to hang onto her partner drives him away.

Figure 10
JEALOUSY ICEBERG

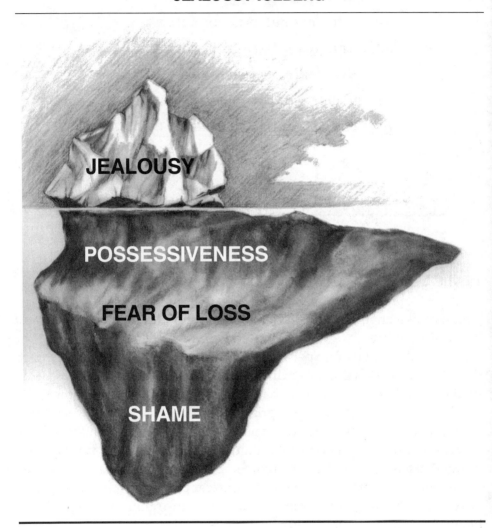

Prescription for Jealousy

If you are the jealous person, make it a rule to talk about the fear each time you talk about the something you feel your partner has done to make you jealous. This may prevent your partner from pulling away from you. It may also, over time, reduce the fear. Remember, even though it *feels* like she is making you jealous and afraid, it's really your own fears that are causing the problem.

> *He who catches the bird*
> *catches not the bird's flight.*
>
> *Maria Marcus*

If Your Partner is Jealous

- Do not change your behavior. Your behavior is not the problem—changing it only adds fuel to the fire since she will feel that you wouldn't have changed if there was no reason to.
- Give one, and only one, explanation when you are accused of doing something wrong.
- Use the Broken Record Technique to address the underlying fear. Repeat each time, I know you are afraid of losing me. I care about you. This is not going to happen.
- Do not attempt to reason her out of her feelings. In this particular area she is not sane and attempts to change her are fruitless and will only make you feel frustrated and angry.
- Be aware that helping an insecure, shamed person is a very slow process and you may have to repeat this routine for several years before you make an appreciable dent.
- When an episode has passed, talk about your own injury at being mistrusted without cause and the damage the accusations are causing in your relationship. Encourage her to get professional help.
- Be aware that you are choosing to end the intimacy in your relationship if you respond to the accusations by feeling like "I have the name, I might as well have the game". Few relationships can survive that kind of betrayal and it is unlikely that you can ever recapture the closeness and trust that was once there.

Small amounts of jealousy need not create problems. Our language sets us up to be jealous—we talk about my husband or my wife, etc. This feeling can foster a sense of security and some protection. Unfortunately, all too often jealousy takes one over like a cancer that eats away the best parts of the relationship.

STEPCHILDREN

There are few challenges in life more formidable than the formation of a blended family. Look at the recipe:

Take several individuals with varying degrees of maturity—some adults, some children, some adults feeling and acting like children, some children feeling and acting like adults. Each person is coping in an individual way with grief. Since step-families are founded on a loss, each participant must cope with all the familiar grief emotions—shock, denial, rage, blame, bargaining, acceptance.

Add to this mix a major change requiring the addition of new coping skills to deal with issues like loyalty, jealousy, and fairness.

Throw in a liberal dash of "normal" parent-child stresses and a pinch of new couple adjustment problems. Coat it all with a thick dusting of unrealistic hopes and expectations.

Daunting prospect, isn't it?

Many factors will interact to influence the process of blending, so each new step-family has to find its own way. There are, however, some commonalities:

- Most parents are very bonded to their children and have intense feelings about how they should be raised. Differences between you and your partner or between you and the children's father can easily be experienced as criticism and reacted to defensively. The non-custodial parent may feel threatened at the further loss of his children and may become hypersensitive to any move he may interpret as your trying to further alienate his children from him.
- Most children are very bonded to their parents, no matter how inadequate the parenting may have been or continues to be. As a result, they may develop intense loyalties and may feel that any attachment to you is a betrayal of the natural parent.
- Your children may react to their loss of exclusive right to you by experiencing your efforts to form a relationship with the stepchildren as abandonment of them.
- All of the "normal" stresses and strains between parents and children may tend to become filtered through the "step" lens.
- You may have difficulty accepting that your partner will always have a relationship with the children's father.

Guidelines for New Families

- Expect difficulties. Be patient with yourself and your partner, the ex, and all the kids. Forming a new family with pieces of broken families takes time (some estimate four-seven years), care, and understanding.
- Make your relationship with your partner the priority—this can become the foundation to build on. In addition, all children develop best in homes where the adults are solidly connected.
- Model the behavior you want from the others. Choose your actions to accomplish this, rather than reacting to the behaviors directed at you.
- Set boundaries, accept no abuse. Allow each party to establish his own relationship to the others. Don't attempt to break bonds or force attachments. Ask yourself "Whose problem is it?" before you intervene.
- Be willing to accept that you may always be unappreciated and unloved.
- Always aim for understanding rather than agreement.
- Acknowledge the difficulties for everyone while keeping the faith that you can do it.

> *One of the most difficult things*
> *everyone has to learn is that*
> *for your entire life you*
> *must "Keep Fighting" and*
> *adjusting if you hope to survive.*
>
> George H. Allen

INFIDELITY

It is the style these days to be very blasé about infidelity. Books and articles have been written proclaiming that such betrayals are common, that they don't necessarily mean anything, that they can make a marriage better, and that they promote a healthy independence. We suspect it is not a coincidence that these are the voices of the perpetrators, one does not hear much about the benefits of *being* betrayed.

> *"That which is without is a reflection of that which is within. If there is chaos in your private world, look within, for there is chaos there also."*
>
> Voice of Silence

A person *chooses* to betray his partner. Sometimes many small choices lead to the betrayal—sometimes it's a momentary lapse, taking advantage of someone immediately available. There are probably as many reasons given for making such a choice as there are offenders. Some common reasons are:

- sexual dissatisfaction with your partner
- an addiction to excitement, needing new sexual partners
- a means to ending the marriage
- a belief that if one is attracted to someone, he needs her
- feeling inadequate, needing to prove oneself
- fear that life is passing one by
- fear of intimacy; a means of keeping distance and/or limiting the relationship
- inability to get one's needs met in the marriage
- a need to feel attractive or desirable
- a belief that an extramarital affair is just sex—it means nothing about one's feelings for his marriage or partner
- a means of punishing one's partner

The betrayer may feel:

- guilty
- worried about being discovered
- afraid of losing his partner
- anger at his partner for being so depriving that he had to look elsewhere to get his needs met
- a loss of self-esteem
- a loss of self-respect
- untrustworthy
- relief because he is desirable and or good enough sexually
- very little—insisting that the betrayal means nothing

The depth of injury to the betrayer may thus range from being relatively minor to severe, depending on the level of his integrity.

The wounds for the betrayed are predictably more serious. She is likely to feel that:

- her ability to trust (you, the relationship, herself, any future partner) has been severely damaged
- you don't value her or the relationship
- you are not committed to her or the relationship
- you are not loyal to her or the relationship
- your have no integrity or trustworthiness
- you do not love her
- you are unhappy with her
- she is no longer special to you
- she is unattractive, inadequate, undesirable, worthless
- her pride has been wounded
- she has become humiliated
- she has lost something valuable
- you have intentionally deeply injured her

No surface wounds here, only major injuries that may never adequately heal.

The most likely resolution to a betrayal is a divorce, either immediately after the discovery or after a destructive delay. During this period the betrayed partner's anger may surface in revenge affairs, an intense desire to hurt the perpetrator, withholding of forgiveness, coldness or withdrawal, or using the information in a never-ending attempt to punish.

Rebuilding after infidelity is possible. It requires that both parties are willing and able to tolerate repeated cycles of anger and pain.

> *Both the hummingbird and the vulture fly over the nation's deserts.*
>
> *All vultures see is rotting meat, because that is what they look for. They thrive on that diet.*
>
> *But hummingbirds ignore the smelly flesh of dead animals. Instead, they look for the colorful blossoms of desert plants.*
>
> *The vultures live on what was. They live on the past. They fill themselves with what is dead and gone.*
>
> *But hummingbirds live on what is. They seek new life. They fill themselves with freshness and life.*
>
> *Each bird finds what it is looking for. We all do.*
>
> *Steve Goodier*

The Offender Needs To:

- be willing to acknowledge that he made a destructive choice
- be genuinely sorry
- acknowledge the pain and rage his partner endured and understand that these will return in cycles for a long time
- recognize that the mistrust his partner feels is not jealously but the logical reaction to being betrayed
- risk being vulnerable so he can get his needs met with his partner

The Betrayed Partner Needs To:

- allow the wound to heal with cycles of forgiveness
- move past the victim role by recognizing that she is making choices
- shift to a no-fault pattern—assigning blame only causes more injury
- come to understand that the betrayal was a statement about her partner's level of integrity, not about her lovability

The Couple Must:

- identify and work on unresolved problems
- make a contract to hang tough during the healing cycles
- focus on the good things they share
- review ways to please each other and to show caring for each other
- draw up a plan for rebuilding trust
- be patient with each other and the process
- understand that the relationship may become valuable and worthwhile *and* that it will never be the same again

When one looks at the whole picture, not just the impact on the offender, the true cost of infidelity is staggering.

DEPRESSION

One-third to one-half of all the men in our groups test out as clinically depressed. Depression is a factor in domestic violence in several ways:

- The depressed person has little energy to work on life's normal problems so these tend to get larger and worse over time. This, in turn, increases the stress for both people.
- Studies have shown that the major cause of marital dissatisfaction is not the negative interactions (such as fights) but the lack of positive interactions. Studies also show that one of the effects of depression is the cessation of positive interactions. So, the depressed person stops doing positive things in the relationship, marital dissatisfaction increases and the likelihood of more fights increases.
- Depression lowers the levels of some of the brain neurotransmitters, including serotonin, the impulse-control chemical.

Clinical depression is different from the normal depression we all feel when things go wrong. Everyone's life has ups and downs. The downs which we may call being depressed are situational depression—they improve when our situations improve. Situational depression can be sudden, as sometimes happens following an unexpected major loss. You can work yourself out of this type of depression by forcing yourself to exercise and to go out to do social things.

Clinical depression is much more serious. It can lead to suicide if left untreated. The clinically depressed person suffers from brain chemistry changes which affect the way he feels, behaves, and thinks. The clinically depressed person suffers major energy losses, his appetite and sleep patterns may be disrupted, he begins to isolate himself and he may experience intense spells of hopelessness and despair.

Women who are clinically depressed generally get help because they look and act depressed. This is the woman who wakes up exhausted and then drags around the house tired all day. As the depression deepens, she may begin to cry frequently and to express feelings that she (and everyone else) would be better off if she were dead. In most cases, family members become alarmed and insist that she get help.

Clinically depressed men may not show that they are heading into trouble. Most of them go to work every day, come home, do what they have to do and almost imperceptibly slip into a very deep mudhole that they are unable to climb out of. One of the most insidious aspects of such depression is that the man himself may not recognize that anything is wrong. The process is so gradual that he doesn't notice.

If you think you or your partner may be depressed, see your family doctor for an assessment. There are some very effective medications that can help you get your life back. Anti-depressants are not mood-elevators, nor are they addictive. Most people need only a few months on them to recover. Don't let your fear keep you from getting help.

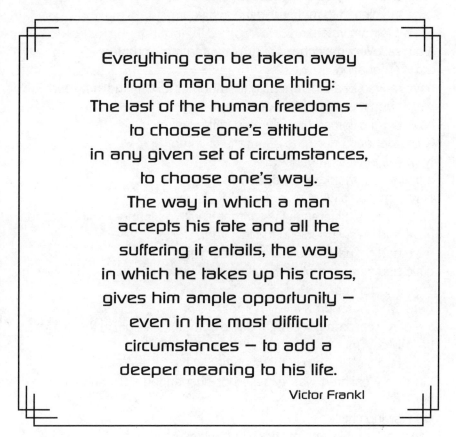

Everything can be taken away
from a man but one thing:
The last of the human freedoms –
to choose one's attitude
in any given set of circumstances,
to choose one's way.
The way in which a man
accepts his fate and all the
suffering it entails, the way
in which he takes up his cross,
gives him ample opportunity –
even in the most difficult
circumstances – to add a
deeper meaning to his life.

Victor Frankl

STRESS

Stress plays major role in domestic violence. We've already told you that the anger chemicals in your body are the same as the stress chemicals—so you may be primed for anger all the time. The most common characteristic of men in our groups is their very high stress level. Look at this checklist of stressors.

Figure 11
STRESSORS CHECKLIST

- [ ] I am under 30 years old.
- [ ] I am between 40 and 50 years old.
- [ ] I belong to a minority racial group.
- [ ] I have been arrested in the last year.
- [ ] Someone closed to me died in the last year.
- [ ] I am a Vietnam veteran.
- [ ] I am a recovering alcoholic or am in a treatment program.
- [ ] I am on probation.
- [ ] I have moved to a different neighborhood or town in the last year.
- [ ] I have been married less than 10 years.
- [ ] I have been divorced or separated in the last year.
- [ ] My partner and I disagree about the children.
- [ ] My wife is a full-time housewife.
- [ ] I make all the major family decisions.
- [ ] My wife makes all the major family decisions.
- [ ] I have had a big increase in arguments with my partner in the last year.
- [ ] I have had in-law trouble in the last year.
- [ ] I have had sexual difficulties in the last year.
- [ ] I have had serious problems with the health or behavior of a family member in the last year.
- [ ] There are stepchildren in my home.
- [ ] One of my children got caught doing something illegal in the last year.
- [ ] I have two or more children.
- [ ] I have had a child born in the last year.
- [ ] One of my children was expelled or suspended from school in the last year.
- [ ] I work swing shift.
- [ ] I have had trouble with my boss in the last year.
- [ ] I have had trouble with people at work in the last year.
- [ ] There has been a big increase in the hours worked or the responsibility on the job in the last year.
- [ ] I am a manual worker.
- [ ] I was laid off or fired in the last year.
- [ ] I have had a mortgage or loan foreclosed in the last year.
- [ ] I am employed part-time or am unemployed.
- [ ] My partner is very worried about our economic security.
- [ ] Our family income is under $17,000 per year.

How many apply to you? Can you add even more? Studies indicate a very high correlation between the number of major stressors and the probability of domestic violence. The trick is not to get rid of the stressors (impossible in most cases), but to respond to them differently. The most common recommendations are:

- Take up regular physical exercise to pull your body chemistry back in line.
- Talk with your partner about the stresses in your lives. Knowing how pressured each of you is may allow you to cut each other some slack.
- Make relaxation time for both of you a priority. When was the last time the two of you went out, without the kids, to do one of the fun things you did while you were dating?

There are many good books and programs on stress reduction. Pick one and follow the advice. Excess stress can kill relationships, and people.

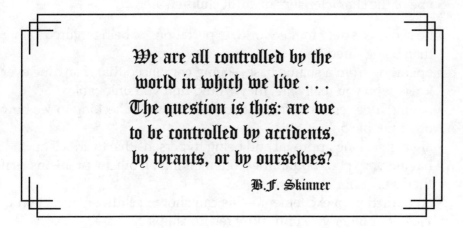

We are all controlled by the
world in which we live . . .
The question is this: are we
to be controlled by accidents,
by tyrants, or by ourselves?

B.F. Skinner

ADULT CHILDREN

Adult children are people whose parents were alcoholics, mentally ill, abusive, or neglectful. Because the parents' problems were so extreme, they could not meet some of their children's basic needs. These children grew up with major developmental areas which do not keep pace with their chronological age—areas which, in effect, do not "grow up". Many of these adults have behaviors that are an attempt to get these needs met, or are childlike emotional reactions.

> # We do not see things as they are. We see them as we are.
>
> The Talmud

Some of the characteristics of adult children are:

- no sense of safety in the world; expectations of being injured rather than being cared for
- operating from a shame base—being convinced that if anyone ever knew who you really are, they would find you unlovable
- having little sense of what is "normal"; always checking to see how other people do it
- always seeking approval and being hypersensitive to criticism
- having very poor boundaries, often taking on others' problems as if they were your own
- an addiction to excitement—this can show itself in an attraction to violent or otherwise unhealthy relationships
- inability to experience or express feelings
- being reactive rather than proactive in the world

As you can see from this list, the skills needed to form healthy relationships are not developed, causing major difficulties when adult children marry. It is very common for adult children to marry each other.

There are many good books designed to help adult children grow up. (Check the addictions and recovery section of your bookstore.) There is also an excellent organization called Adult Children of Alcoholics (ACOA) which consists of adult children helping each other overcome the handicaps caused by inadequate parenting.

Courage is the price that life
expects for granting peace.

Amelia Earhart

HOSTILITY

Do you hold grudges? Have a short fuse? Blow up easily? Have a quick temper? When you think of certain people, do you clench your teeth (or your fists) and remember how much you hate them? "Yes" answers are an indication that you are accumulating a stockpile of hostility.

Imagine that you saved all your garbage for a year or two—and that you now have to carry it with you wherever you go. Those who choose to store hostility are just like that: handicapped by garbage from the past. Why would anyone choose this as a solution? How does that happen? The process is very similar to another analogy:

> Imagine that a child has fallen and scraped his knee on the sidewalk. He comes in crying—wanting a bandage. He does *not* want his father to pick out the little stones or to clean out the dirt. He knows that touching the wound will hurt more; he has no understanding that not cleaning the wound will ultimately make it worse. His parent would never consider leaving the wound dirty. He knows it would fester up, become more and more tender, and that the infection could eventually spread and poison the child's system.

We choose hostility for the same reason. The child within us wants to avoid the pain of cleaning out a wound. This choice does make the injury very tender and it can become toxic, poisoning our relationships and our selves. Another solution that becomes a problem.

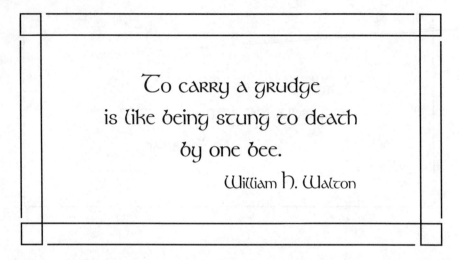

To carry a grudge
is like being stung to death
by one bee.

William H. Walton

It is a very natural human response to react to injury with rage. It's part of the "fight or flight" response we talked about earlier. It's also natural for us to move on to the pain, once the immediate threat is gone. For example, a man in the heat of battle may not even notice that he is injured. After the battle is over, he then becomes aware of the wound and the attendant pain. Some of us refuse to do that generally—because we are afraid the pain will overwhelm us. This refusal keeps us "stuck" in the hating. This not only prevents healing, it allows the wound to fester and may, over time, poison the entire system. It also keeps us tied to the person who injured us.

If your hostility is putting you in jeopardy of being arrested, you might want to consider taking up some form of *strenuous* physical exercise; something like handball or racquetball, something that leaves you physically whipped. It may help keep you out of trouble while you work on reducing the stockpile; however, this is not a long-term solution. The way to do that is a process called forgiveness.

HOSTILITY ILLUSTRATION

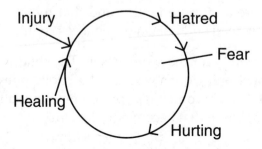

If you are ready to get "unstuck": the next time the rage comes, accept it and do not keep yourself there by fueling the anger with name-calling, vows to hate that SOB forever, etc. As the anger fades, allow yourself to experience the pain. Initially, you may be able to accept the pain for only brief moments. Accept that and know the healing has begun.

FORGIVENESS

We are not talking about the type of forgiveness where you go to someone and "forgive" them for causing an injury. The forgiveness we are talking about is an internal process which cleans out the wounds so they can heal. This type of forgiveness is not about "forgiving and forgetting." In the first place, you can't forget unless you sustain some brain damage that kills brain cells—nor should you. If you put your hand on a hot stove, it is very useful for you to remember what happened. Likewise, if someone hurts you, you should remember; otherwise, you could be trapped in a relationship where someone injures you repeatedly. This forgiveness also is not a way of saying that what happened is all right. Injuring people is not all right. Sometimes a man hangs onto his hatred so he can "show that guy" vowing to hate him until the day he dies.

Of course, such a response means that you are carrying the garbage around while the object of your hatred has gone on with his life. Something a little strange about that solution...This type of forgiveness is also not about resuming the relationship. You can do this forgiving without ever seeing or speaking to the person again. Resuming a relationship with someone who repeatedly injures or betrays you makes little sense.

There is a cycle to the forgiveness we are talking about. It looks like this:

HEALING CYCLE

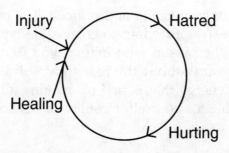

Forgiveness is generally not a one-time event. Imagine that people have layers—just like an onion. A minor injury, like an insult from a stranger, may damage only the outer layer which could require only one forgiveness cycle.

ONION ILLUSTRATION #1

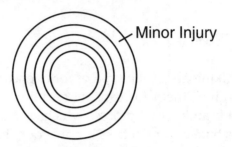

A major injury, like being betrayed by your partner, may wound many layers and will require many cycles of forgiveness. The healing that is part of each cycle makes it possible for you to deal with the rage and pain of the next cycle.

ONION ILLUSTRATION #2

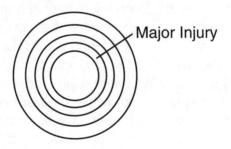

As the cycle repeats, the parts will gradually become balanced out. Eventually the wound will heal, leaving a scar which is experienced as sadness.

Forgiveness can be frightening and difficult. The benefit is that elusive notion called *freedom*. Freedom to choose the type of relationship you will have with the person who injured you (if any). Freedom to allow others near you without the fear they will bump the injury. Freedom to use the energy that is tied up hauling all the old garbage around for a better life for yourself. Hostility or freedom? The choice is yours.

Two special notes about the *forgiveness* process (necessary, because human beings have an absolute genius for complicating **everything**).

HURTING ILLUSTRATION

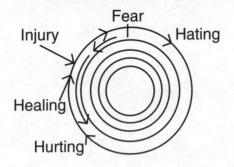

First, it is possible to skip the hating and get stuck in the hurting. This can happen when a person cannot accept the part of him that hates, because he is afraid. The fear could be that in his rage he will destroy someone else or himself, or that he will become just like the perpetrator. This is the man who will tell you that he knows he needs to let go of the woman who repeatedly betrays him, but he can't. If you are "stuck" in the hurting, the trick is to drive the process backwards. (It works just as well in either direction.)

Second, the healing of any major injury is much easier with help from someone who understands and supports the process. Friends, family, your minister, your sponsor, groups like VietNam Veterans Outreach or ACOA—people who care make the process less long and lonely. If you were abused as a child, it is possible that this process did not develop—just as a seed without water does not grow. A good therapist will provide the water and the sun's warmth so you become the person you were meant to be. Choose to come alive...get some help.

If you're defending all the time,
you are pushing away life, and
the life you are pushing away
is your own.

Merle Shain

SECTION IV
HEALING CHOICES

ABUSIVE BEHAVIORS

Just what is abuse anyway? There are many definitions of abuse and violence. The one here is that abuse is any chosen behavior that damages your partner, yourself, or your relationship. Abusive behaviors can be categorized in many different ways. For the purposes of this book, we have broken them into four types—violent, hurtful, controlling and disconnecting.

We define as violent those behaviors which are intended to make our partners afraid. Choices that are hurtful are intended to cause our partners pain. Behaviors which are controlling are intended to change our partner against her will. The choices that are disconnecting to the relationship are abusive because of the expectations inherent in the relationship. Many behaviors overlap categories; in addition, definitions of pain and fear can be somewhat subjective. Feel free to redefine or recategorize any of them to fit your experience. Most of these behaviors were elicited from men who are recovering in the groups we facilitate for abusive behavior.

In the figures that follow, check off the behaviors that have been experienced by one or both of you in this relationship.

Figure 12
VIOLENT BEHAVIORS—Behaviors That Evoke Fear

- ☐ hitting
- ☐ burning
- ☐ kicking
- ☐ choking
- ☐ pushing
- ☐ raping
- ☐ punching
- ☐ throwing things
- ☐ assaulting with things or weapons
- ☐ destroying things
- ☐ injuring pets or children
- ☐ physical intimidation (menacing)
- ☐ threatening physical violence
- ☐ refusing to let go of the partner
- ☐ refusing to leave when asked to
- ☐ physical confinement (not being allowed to leave)

- ☐ physical restraint (not being allowed to move)
- ☐ forcing the partner to use drugs or alcohol
- ☐ threatening to take the children
- ☐ standing threateningly close
- ☐ jabbing
- ☐ pulling hair
- ☐ pinching
- ☐ throwing bodily
- ☐ picking up the person and moving her
- ☐ forcing sexual activity
- ☐ spanking

Figure 13
HURTFUL BEHAVIORS—Behaviors That Evoke Pain

- ☐ criticizing (of one's self, one's actions, one's looks, one's gender)
- ☐ name-calling
- ☐ swearing at
- ☐ mocking
- ☐ putting down
- ☐ ridiculing
- ☐ accusations
- ☐ blaming
- ☐ making legal threats
- ☐ disparaging the partner's opinions
- ☐ making all of the major decisions
- ☐ not supporting the partner in disputes with others
- ☐ insulting
- ☐ instilling guilt
- ☐ belittling
- ☐ shaming
- ☐ making the partner feel stupid
- ☐ bring up the past to hurt
- ☐ pointing out the partner's weaknesses
- ☐ not supporting the partner's personal growth
- ☐ embarrassing the partner
- ☐ laughing at the partner

Figure 14—CONTROLLING BEHAVIORS
Behaviors Intended to Change the Partner's Behavior

- [ ] interrupting
- [ ] changing the topic
- [ ] shouting
- [ ] not responding
- [ ] pressuring
- [ ] rushing
- [ ] being impatient
- [ ] guilt-tripping
- [ ] sulking or pouting
- [ ] playing the innocent victim
- [ ] isolating the partner
- [ ] threatening to commit suicide
- [ ] threatening to report the partner to the authorities
- [ ] treating the partner like a servant
- [ ] refusing to talk about problems
- [ ] stamping out of the room, slamming out of the house
- [ ] crying
- [ ] monitoring the partner's time—want an accounting for every minute
- [ ] being rude to partner's family or friends
- [ ] discouraging the partner's friendships
- [ ] demanding obedience
- [ ] not allowing the partner to work or go to school
- [ ] restricting the use of the car
- [ ] restricting the use of the phone
- [ ] being sarcastic
- [ ] nagging or bitching
- [ ] responding with a disgusted or judgmental tone of voice
- [ ] withholding support or encouragement
- [ ] saying "I told you so"
- [ ] being inconsistent
- [ ] ignoring the partner
- [ ] forcing the partner to choose between you and extended family
- [ ] playing the martyr
- [ ] refusing to negotiate
- [ ] refusing to provide adequate financial support
- [ ] not paying the bills

- ☐ taking the partner's money without permission
- ☐ spending family money on drugs and alcohol
- ☐ making the partner ask for money
- ☐ being stingy with money given to the partner
- ☐ compulsive spending
- ☐ gambling
- ☐ credit card addiction

Figure 15—DISCONNECTING BEHAVIORS
Behaviors Damaging to the Relationship

- ☐ allowing one's partner to be abusive
- ☐ affairs, flirting, talking about the attractiveness of others
- ☐ forced sex accomplished by emotional blackmail
- ☐ withholding sex to express anger and maintain control
- ☐ irrational mood swings
- ☐ not respecting one's partner
- ☐ emotional withholding:
    - ☐ not expressing feelings
    - ☐ not giving praise, attention, support, concern, validation
    - ☐ not being vulnerable
- ☐ breaking promises
- ☐ not taking care of oneself
- ☐ blaming one's addiction on the partner
- ☐ snooping
- ☐ mistrusting
- ☐ lying
- ☐ revealing personal information the partner does not want known
- ☐ intruding on the partner's private time
- ☐ failing to respect the partner's needs
- ☐ being insensitive to the partner's feelings
- ☐ giving the partner the silent treatment
- ☐ refusing to accept apologies
- ☐ picking a fight
- ☐ failing to include the partner in plans or activities
- ☐ failing to put the partner first
- ☐ being inconsiderate
- ☐ not putting a priority on the relationship

☐ not sharing one's life with one's partner
☐ being too busy for one's partner
☐ not planning for the future so one's partner is insecure
☐ taking one's partner for granted
☐ not discussing events that damage the relationship

These lists are certainly not exhaustive. There appears to be no end to the ways we can choose to be abusive. There are four points we would like to make about abusive behaviors:

- They are *choices*. No one can force you to behave abusively. You must make the choice each time.
- They are very *ineffective* ways to get what you want. If you are angry at your partner, it is likely that you feel she has injured you. What you want is for her to acknowledge your injury, assure you she did not intend to injure you, and work with you to find ways to keep if from happening again. If you get up in her face, yell and scream at her, call her names and push her hot buttons, it's *very* unlikely that she will respond by reaching out to you and apologizing. We have this goofy notion that if we make our partners feel like shit, they will somehow become more loving. Ludicrous, isn't it?
- Every time we choose to be abusive to our partner, we set in motion a psychological process which results in *dehumanization*. In order for us to live with our choices, we begin to make our victim less of a person. An extreme example of this is that it's far easier to shoot a "slant-eyed gook" than it is to kill another person. This is one of the factors that make it easier to become more abusive over time.
- Each abusive choice *damages* you. Choosing abusive behaviors erodes your self-esteem, another factor that causes abusiveness to escalate. Your partner can always choose to leave you—you take your self-esteem with you wherever you go.

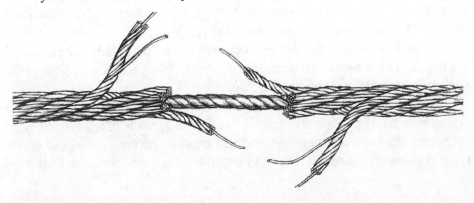

AUTHENTIC CHOICES

At times when we finish looking at the abusive behaviors, one of the men will comment that if all of this is removed from his relationship, there would be nothing left. We suspect this is an exaggeration; however many of us did not grow up in places where we saw much authentic behavior. (Authentic behavior is acting in ways that reflect our best selves.) We have developed a model to explain what such behaviors look like.

Figure 16
AUTHENTIC BEHAVIORS MODEL

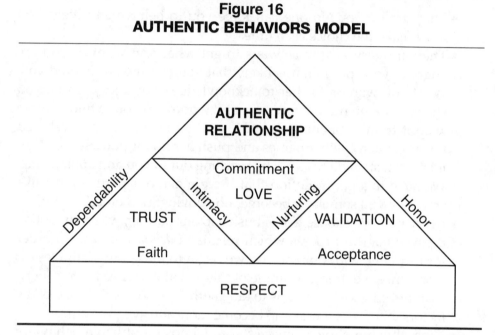

One of the components necessary for an authentic relationship is TRUST. It's hard to imagine you could have a real relationship with someone you don't trust—or if you're not a trustworthy person. *Dependability* is one of the components of trust. Dependability doesn't just mean that when you say you'll do something, you do it; it also means the two of you can depend on each other to be there when things get rough. There is also an element of predictability—some of your partner's behaviors should be predictable.

The *intimacy* component is the element of sharing the deeper, more vulnerable parts of yourself. Each of us has a "public face" we show to everyone. It's hard to imagine we could trust someone if we don't know what is behind that mask. The *faith* component means we trust in things

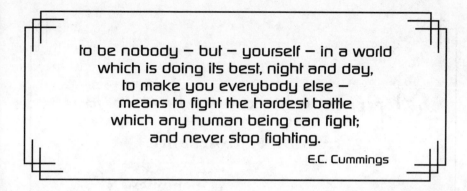

to be nobody – but – yourself – in a world
which is doing its best, night and day,
to make you everybody else –
means to fight the hardest battle
which any human being can fight;
and never stop fighting.

E.C. Cummings

we cannot prove. We spend significant amounts of time apart, we cannot prove we are not betraying each other in our times apart, we do have faith in each other and our relationship.

We understand VALIDATION as the process of caring about another person as he is. The *nurturing* component is there because none of us is grown-up all the time. Everyone occasionally needs someone to hold him and taken care of him. *Honoring* is putting our partners first and letting them and other people know that. *Acceptance* is giving our partners the gift of acceptance of things about them we might wish were different. Acceptance is *not* stuffing. Real acceptance builds no resentment.

The LOVE component is not the same as "being in love". Being in love is a feeling. It's wonderful and we all would like to be in love all the time. If that were possible, we'd probably be living in caves, as little work would be done. Like all feelings, being in love passes—that's where real love clicks in. Real love is a decision you make. It has the intimacy and nurturing components and a large dollop of commitment— commitment to behave in loving ways even when we don't feel "in love".

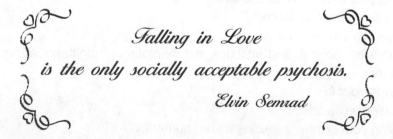

Falling in Love
is the only socially acceptable psychosis.

Elvin Semrad

This entire model rests on a base of RESPECT. Respect is a basic attitude through which all the other behaviors are expressed. If you are always respectful to your partner, you won't go far wrong.

A person who knows how to love cannot be controlled.

Anonymous

The following list has been generated over time by the men in our groups. How many of these authentic behaviors are a regular part of your relationship?

Figure 17—AUTHENTIC BEHAVIORS
Behaviors That Support a Relationship & Promote Both Partners' Growth

- ☐ risking being yourself
- ☐ sharing
- ☐ allowing your partner to share your experience
- ☐ talking things over with your partner
- ☐ being honest
- ☐ listening
- ☐ telling your partner what you want
- ☐ expressing your feelings
- ☐ speaking up when injured
- ☐ expressing feelings and attitudes, not opinions or judgments about your partner
- ☐ sharing your fears
- ☐ touching while talking
- ☐ valuing your partner's frailties as her humanity
- ☐ kindness
- ☐ tenderness
- ☐ being sensitive to your partner's feelings and needs

- [ ] being appreciative
- [ ] making allowances for your partner's moods and upsets
- [ ] making unexpected gestures or giving unexpected gifts
- [ ] wanting more for your partner because you care
- [ ] caressing
- [ ] stroking
- [ ] holding
- [ ] fixing your partner's favorite foods
- [ ] focusing on what's right with your partner, rather than her faults
- [ ] giving massages
- [ ] standing guard over your partner's vulnerabilities
- [ ] encouraging your partner's growth even if it frightens you
- [ ] helping your partner increase her capacity to relate
- [ ] encouraging your partner to be herself, no matter what others think
- [ ] rejoicing and celebrating her triumphs
- [ ] helping her over the rough spots or mistakes
- [ ] helping her with the chores
- [ ] being enthusiastic about your partner's growth
- [ ] doing what your partner asks whenever possible
- [ ] being patient
- [ ] responding to bad moods with affection
- [ ] writing "I love you" notes
- [ ] planning pleasant surprises
- [ ] cherishing
- [ ] confirming your partner's experience
- [ ] letting your partner know you are happy to be with her
- [ ] being responsive to her
- [ ] letting her know when she moves you
- [ ] valuing your partner's differences
- [ ] giving flowers, gifts, compliments
- [ ] being tolerant
- [ ] showing that you love her for who she is, not what she does
- [ ] being forgiving
- [ ] behaving authentically, even when you don't feel like it
- [ ] giving your partner the freedom to be herself
- [ ] "giving up" as a gift
- [ ] having faith in her judgment
- [ ] being unwilling to live a lie
- [ ] keeping your partner's secrets
- [ ] being congruent

- ☐ being truthful and kind
- ☐ telling the whole truth, not a slanted version
- ☐ be willing to hear your partner's reasons if she breaks her word
- ☐ giving your partner your best
- ☐ making time for your partner
- ☐ being willing to make sacrifices
- ☐ being there in times of sadness or hurt
- ☐ investing your time, energy, thoughts, patience, and feelings
- ☐ promising to remain in the relationship even when problems arise
- ☐ be willing to consider partner's needs before making a decision
- ☐ making joint financial decisions
- ☐ be willing to compromise
- ☐ cooperating
- ☐ being flexible
- ☐ developing mutual interests
- ☐ presenting a united front with others
- ☐ not playing tit-for-tat
- ☐ doing a secret service for your partner each day
- ☐ creating a safe atmosphere
- ☐ sharing your daily life
- ☐ arranging time to be alone together
- ☐ doing only those things which are good for the relationship and the two people involved
- ☐ being considerate
- ☐ being loyal
- ☐ speaking only well of your partner in public
- ☐ being attentive to your partner in public
- ☐ prizing your partner
- ☐ treating you partner with dignity
- ☐ treating you partner as your best friend

Again, these lists are not exhaustive. People can be wonderfully creative when it comes to authentic behaviors. These behaviors are all CHOICES. You can always choose to behave authentically, no matter how the other person is treating you. Behaving authentically toward someone is the most likely way to get someone to treat you authentically. Finally, you cannot lose if you make authentic choices, for no matter what the other person does, you can walk away feeling good about yourself.

We teach other people how to treat us, principally by the way we treat them. What we get back from our relationships is a direct reflection of what we put in.

Given that we feel good when we are authentic, and such behaviors are the most probable way to generate loving behavior, why don't we behave authentically all the time? The answer is that we are afraid. Afraid of being rejected. Afraid of failing. Afraid of being abandoned by the people we depend on. Afraid that others will discover our shame.

FEAR & SHAME

Most of our lives are driven by fear. Our attempts to cope with the many fears that lurk in each of us can drastically limit our choices. There are two common ways to deal with fears—attempting to deaden them or trying to control them.

Those who choose to deaden fear are often driven to self-destructive actions. The addictive behaviors fall into this category. The other major solution, control, drives many to choose abusive behaviors which are designed to control others. Both these choices fail in the long run because the consequences set up a vicious circle.

The fear is actually generated by a shame base. Shame is not the feeling you have when you have *done* something wrong. Shame is a deep, gut-level sense that *you* are wrong—that you are unlovable, not good enough, that if anyone *really* knew, they would leave you. The deadening and controlling behaviors *feed* the shame base, making it larger. As it grows, it generates more fear, which then requires more deadening or controlling, or both. Round and round it goes, growing more extreme with each cycle.

Shame is a part of most of us, but it's not all we are. Each of us also has a loving, caring part more central to who we are than even shame. These two parts operate in *inverse* proportion to each other—increasing one makes the other smaller. We need both parts. Having shame allows us to empathize and understand how others can make abusive choices. Love and caring allows us to be our best selves. Each of us is capable of choosing which part to feed. We are feeding the shame when we make abusive choices and feeding the love and caring when we make authentic choices.

The following figure shows the consequences of our choices.

Figure 18
CHOICES FLOW CHART

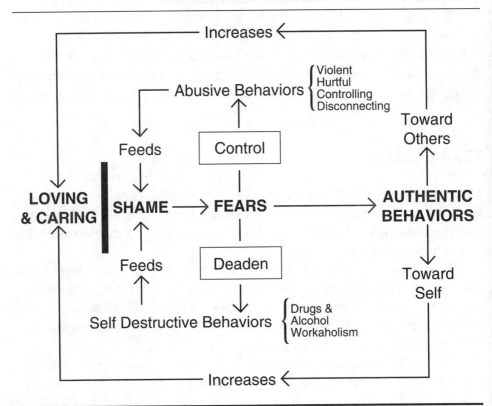

If you decide to begin making more authentic choices, you'll find it difficult at first. As your loving, caring part grows, such choices become easier and easier to make. These choices not only determine how you behave, but ultimately who *you* are.

∽∾∽∾   ∽∾∽∾

... man or woman becomes fully human
only by his or her choices and his or her
commitment to them. People attain worth and
dignity by the multitude of decisions
they make from day to day.
These decisions require courage.

Rollo May

Figure 19
HOW WE BRING OUR WORST FEARS TO OUR DOOR

FEAR	MASK	ACTION	RESULT
losing partner	jealousy	possessiveness	loses partner
abandonment	controlling position	pushing	is abandoned
rejection	protecting myself	putting up walls acting indifferent Who needs you?	is rejected
being a sucker	standing up for my rights	withholding caring	becomes a lover
helplessness powerlessness	aggression depression	violence withdrawal	becomes helpless or powerless
ridicule	being right	justifies attacks	invites ridicule
intimacy	manufacture something wrong with partner	withdraw start arguments numb out with drugs/alcohol	loss of intimacy
loss of control of self	need to control others	controlling behaviors	drives partner away
failure	don't care workaholic	dead end life no energy for partner	relationship fails
sexual inadequacy	bragging equating force with prowess	forced sexual activity	drives partner away
women	macho attitude	womanizing putting women down	invites hateful responses

We will close this book be reprinting the words to a wonderful song and a quotation from a master therapist.

RAZOR'S EDGE

I have danced on the razor's edge.
I have stood trembling on the brink.
I have stared down into the abyss.
Let me tell you what I think.

Chorus:
I think that hell may be overrated.
I've made my own here in my head.
I don't think it's overstated,
When I say there are many worse things than being dead.

I wanted to play at being God,
Sitting up there on my throne.
Passing judgment down on myself,
On me and me alone.

CHORUS

In all that noise I heard a voice calling me back home.
Reminding me I always had a choice,
If I would just let go.
If I would just let go.

CHORUS

Sometimes the fear of the fall,
Is worse than the pain when you land.
Sometimes running away from it all
Is harder than making a stand.
We all must be tested in the fire,
To see what mettle we are made of.
Somewhere in us all lies the desire,
To burn through the hatred to the love.

I don't think peace is simply stated.
I've found a little now in my head.
I think that death may be overrated.
For now I'd always choose life instead,
For now I'd always choose life instead.

Dave Petty

This song is from an album called *Piece of Mind* by an Indianapolis songwriter named Dave Petty.
It can be ordered by sending $12.00 to Dave at P.O. Box 40748, Indianapolis, IN 46240-4074.

It is our hope that you too, will always choose life instead.

Denny and Margy

For me, anything that gives new hope,
new possibilities and new positive feelings
about ourselves
will make us more whole people
and thus more human, real and loving
in our relationships with others,
If enough of this happens,
the world will become a better place
for all of us.

I matter.
You matter.

What goes on between us matters.

Virginia Satir

PERSONAL GROWTH BIBLIOGRAPHY

Durst, G. Michael. *Napkin Notes: On the Art of Living.* The Center for the Art of Living, Evanston, Illinois, 1988.

Hoff, Benjamin. *The Tao of Pooh.* E.P. Button, Inc., New York, New York, 1982.

Kopp, Sheldon B. *If You Meet the Buddha on the Road, Kill Him.* Bantam Books, New York, New York, 1972.

Malone, Thomas Patrick and Malone, Patrick Thomas. *The Art of Intimacy.* Prentice-Hall, New York, New York, 1987.

Paul, Jordan and Paul, Margaret. *From Conflict to Caring.* CompCare Publishers, Minneapolis, Minnesota, 1989.

Pearson, Carol S. *The Hero Within.* Harper & Row, San Francisco, California, 1986.

Prather, High and Prather, Gayle. *Notes to Each Other.* Bantam Books, New York, New York, 1990.

Rusk, Tom and Read, Randy. *I Want to Change But I Don't Know How.* Price/Stern/Sloan, Los Angeles, California, 1986.

Peck, M. Scott. *The Road Less Traveled.* Simon and Shuster, New York, New York, 1978.

Shain, Merle. *Courage My Love.* Bantam Books, New York, New York, 1989.

Tanenbaum, Joe. *Male & Female Realities.* Candle Publishing Company, Sugar Land, Texas, 1989.

Wegscheider-Cruse, Sharon. *Coupleship.* Health Communications, Inc., Deerfield Beach, Florida. 1988.

Covey, Stephen R. *The Seven Habits of Highly Effective People.* Simon and Schuster, New York, New York, 1990.

Malone, Thomas Patrick and Malone, Patrick Thomas. *The Windows of Experience.* Simon & Schuster, New York, New York, 1992.

Josselson, Ruthellen. *The Space Between Us.* Jossey-Bass, Inc., San Francisco, California, 1992.

INDEX

This book was published by

DENTON CONSULTING COMPANY

P.O. Box 247

Loveland, OH 45140

Additional copies may be ordered by sending $20.00 each (includes shipping and handling) to the above address. (Ohio residents must include appropriate sales tax.)

Denton Consulting Company specializes in psychoeducational groups for abusive men. Write for a brochure listing other publications and services.